DISCUSSION BOOKS

General Editors:
Richard Wilson, D.Litt., and A. J. J. Ratcliff, M.A.

❦

ECONOMICS FOR DEMOCRATS

No. 19

ECONOMICS FOR DEMOCRATS

by

GEOFFREY CROWTHER

THOMAS NELSON AND SONS LTD
LONDON EDINBURGH PARIS MELBOURNE
TORONTO AND NEW YORK

First published July 1939
Reprinted 1939, 1940, 1942, 1943,
1944, 1945, 1946, 1947

CONTENTS

PART ONE.—GOALS

PART TWO.—FALSE ROADS

PART THREE.—SIGNPOSTS

PREFACE

" ECONOMICS FOR DEMOCRATS " seemed both to the publishers and to me to be such a good title that it could not be missed. But I must begin with the confession that it is not a literally exact description of this book. In the accepted sense of the word, economics refers to the consistent system of generalizations by which the professors seek to explain the ways in which we are all supplied with the material necessities and luxuries of life. Of economics in this sense you will find little or nothing in this book. Indeed, it is far more a political pamphlet than a textbook, and I devoutly hope that it will not fall into the hands of any economists—not because I am unready to defend my views, with an admixture of professional jargon if necessary, but because the necessity of defending them and of enumerating all the provisos, exceptions, and qualifications to every broadly true statement contained in these pages would occupy so many volumes that we should never be able to get down to brass tacks at all.

Alfred Marshall, the founder of modern British economics, declared that there was no economic statement that was both short and accurate. I am quite sure that is true. It has the unfortunate consequence that any one who tries to write about economics has to choose between being, on the one hand, accurate and intolerably prolix, and, on the other hand, being brief and open to detailed objection. I have deliberately chosen the latter danger. I have tried in this book to cover a very large field and to make my meaning clear. To do this, I have necessarily had to stick to the main road of my argument and ignore the tempting byways. Sometimes, to save time, I have raced along a by-pass and avoided steering my argument round the difficult narrow corners of a congested logical area.

Reader, I beg you to accept my assurance that I am aware of at least some—I hope most—of the qualifications to my forthright statements. I beg you to think what a mess I should have made of the book if I had tried to put them all in. And I beg you to believe me when I say that I have honestly tried to avoid only those by-ways that *are* by-ways, that the road I travel *is* the main road.

G. C.

NOTE TO 1947 REPRINT

Events since 1939 have moved so swiftly that while the main arguments of this book remain unimpaired, actual conditions have substantially changed. However, in general the original text has been preserved, and indeed the conditions described possess a value for the reader by their contrast with those of to-day.

G. C.

PART ONE.—GOALS

ECONOMICS FOR DEMOCRATS

CHAPTER I

WHAT SORT OF ECONOMY?

THIS book is concerned with the democratic reform
of the economic system. It has three parts, each of
which is designed to answer one main question. What
is chiefly wrong with our present economic system?
Why are the chief existing reform movements stepping
off on the wrong foot? What should be the main
principles that a democracy should follow in economic
reform?

Each of these questions is large enough to fill at least
one book. If each of them is to receive more than a nod
of recognition within the covers of one small volume,
we must waste no space in getting down to them.

But there are certain preliminary questions that will
be troublesome unless we get them out of the way first.
So this introductory chapter is devoted to clearing the
ground.

First, what is this " economic system "? Does it exist?

The *Oxford Dictionary* has two main definitions of the
word " system." The first is, " a set or assemblage of
things connected, associated, or interdependent so as to
form a complex unity." The second is, " a whole com-

posed of parts in orderly arrangement, according to some scheme or plan." If we accept the first definition, there certainly is an economic system. The most remarkable thing about the way in which the members of a modern community earn their livings is the amount of unconscious co-operation that is involved. In Great Britain to-day there is not a single man who provides by his own efforts every one of his own wants. Even the most self-sufficient family is dependent upon the co-operation of others for a substantial part of its living. It must make goods for sale to others, or render services to others, or at the very least receive charity from others, in order to be able to purchase some of the elementary necessaries of life. Most people nowadays do not directly supply even a single one of their own wants. The builder, it is true, can (with the assistance of his labourers) provide his own house ; the artist can paint pictures for his own delight ; the musician can provide his own entertainment. But even these are exceptions. Most of us do all our work in a world quite outside our own homes, and buy from others every single thing we consume. When we apply this individual experience to forty-five million people living in one island, and extend it further to the two thousand million people of the world, most of whom are in greater or less degree in the same position of dependence upon and co-operation with the rest of humanity, we must indeed conclude that the economic system is " an assemblage of things interdependent so as to form a complex unity."

The second definition of a system, however, talks about " orderly arrangement " and " some scheme or plan," and by this definition there just as certainly is not an economic system. The complex assemblage of which we were speaking in the last paragraph has in very large part grown up by itself. True, it is not quite comparable to the natural growth of wild flowers or animals, since at every stage in the erection of man's social arrangements the human brain and human desires have played their part in determining the course. But there was no man, or group of men, who, in the beginning, sat down to draw up an orderly scheme or plan according to which all social and economic development was to progress. Even what is known as the capitalist system has been a matter of unconscious growth ; there was no conspiracy of rich men to force on an innocent world a carefully-thought-out system of exploitation. Even in those countries where, in the last few years, the orderly plan has been supposed to be the directive of all activity, the planners have necessarily had to take as their point of departure the unplanned state of affairs they found. They have planned, not the whole economy of the country, but merely the amendments to it.

We can therefore speak of an economic system only if we make it clear to ourselves that it is an organic growth rather than a predetermined system, an assemblage composed of the individual unco-ordinated decisions of countless myriads of individual men, now living and now dead. That does not, of course, mean that Society—which is Man acting in his corporate capacity—has not interfered with the economic system from the start. Every sort of human institution, such as marriage, tribal kinship, religion, and a score of others has had its effect upon the shape of the economic system. Even apart from these unconscious and indirect influences of human organization, there have from the earliest times been conscious and direct interferences with the free flow of the ordinary business of life. The very earliest records of Mesopotamian civilization bear witness to edicts issued in the attempt to influence the course of trade. The price of bread and the rate of usury are two matters which the state has always closely controlled, and in an early stage of economic development the two between them covered a very large part of all economic activity. The nineteenth century of the Christian era was, it is true, much impressed, in a theoretical sort of way, by the doctrine of *laisser-faire*, according to which the interference of Society with the economic system should, on principle, be reduced to a minimum. Even in the nineteenth century, however, there was never complete *laisser-faire*. The state could not completely forbear from interfering, and the indirect influence of human institutions continued, in spite of all the *laisser-faire* preachings, to exert an enormous influence on the way in which men earned and spent their livings.

There is, then, something that can properly be called an economic system, built up partly of Man's unconscious instincts, partly of his deliberate intentions. But it is perhaps necessary to go a little further in description of it. In the modern world, where most of us live in towns, remote from the original source of most of what we consume, and earn our livings at highly specialized jobs, it is a little difficult to conceive of the economic system as a whole. The simplest form of economic organization, barely deserving the name of " system," is the primitive family economy, in which each family unit is entirely self-supporting and self-sufficient. Even when village trades begin to introduce the principle of specialization, and the tinker, the tailor, the candlestick-maker begin to appear, it is still easy to see that each member of the community is labouring to produce a fund of goods upon which all will draw. In a primitive village, cut off by impassable roads from the rest of the country, it is obvious that the consumption of each member of the community depends upon the production of the whole, and that if any one member consumes more than he produces, some other member must be going short.

It is a far cry from such a simple community as that to a complex organism such as our own. We draw on other communities both in space and in time. Every day, every one of us uses things that have been brought for our consumption from the ends of the earth. Every day, every one of us uses things, such as houses, roads, bridges, and all sorts of machinery, provided by people long since dead. That is the consumption side. On the production side, many of us earn our livings by making things that will be consumed abroad, or by constructing new capital equipment whose use will long outlast our lifetime. It is a little difficult for, shall we say, the machine-tool maker to realize in what way he is contributing to the consumption of ordinary families like his own. It is tempting for him to think that, because he never uses a machine-tool in his own home, he has no use for them at all, and that his work is rendered to a vague and alien " economic system " of which he is no part.

But despite all its complications, the modern economic system has, and can only have, the same ulterior purpose as the primitive village community. Specialization and the division of labour are of value only if they help to increase the sum total of goods and services at the disposal of the average consumer. Machine-tools help in the construction of other machines, which make a small part of, say, a motor van which brings bread to your door. When you eat a slice of bread you are consuming not merely the wheat that has gone into it, but infinitely small fractions of the labour of all the men and women who have brought the wheat from the other side of the earth, milled it, baked it, brought it to you ; and of the men and women who have made the machines used in any of those processes, or mined the metal that went into the machines ; and so on in an almost infinite process of specialization.

However indirect and roundabout the methods of production may be, all of them come back in the end to the individual consumer. Perhaps it would be more accurate to say that they *should* come back in the end to the individual consumer, for when the final goods are produced for consumption it may be discovered that the wants of the consumer have been misinterpreted, and that he does not want what has been produced. Or it may be that though he wants the goods that are produced they will do him harm, like noxious drugs, or an excessive consumption of alcohol. Or if they do not do him positive harm, they may be goods whose consumption is merely wasteful and improvident, like many of the things that men and women buy merely to make themselves look fashionable or respectable, or the armaments that states pile up in the effort to be safe. Thus the consumer may make silly mistakes about what he really wants, and the economic system may make equally silly mistakes in interpreting what the consumer does want. But neither fact alters the main principle that the only purpose of the vast complex machinery of production by which all of us earn our livings, and from which all of us derive the necessities of life, is to serve the material needs of the individual citizens of the community.

Much the easiest way of envisaging the economic system is, therefore, to think of it as a vast pool of useful goods and services, to which every citizen contributes (or should contribute), and from which every citizen draws what he wants. There are enormous inequalities in the contributions that each of us makes to the pool ; there are even greater inequalities in the incomes that we draw from the pool. Some of the goods and services put into the pool are not drawn out, and for others there is a greater demand than the pool can satisfy. But these are minor accidents of the working of the system. The community as a whole obviously cannot take out of the pool more than it puts in. On the other hand, if the community has devoted some of its resources to the making of things that are not wanted, they will be left in the pool and the community as a whole will get out less than it has put in. What is more likely is that those people who have been engaged in putting these unwanted goods into the pool will stop putting them in, and failing to find other useful work, will become unemployed. However little the community allows them to draw out of the pool, so long as they remain unemployed they necessarily draw out more than they put in. We have come to learn in recent years that the pool could be considerably increased if every citizen who is ready to contribute to it were able to do so.

This pool is the national income. It is the object of all production, and the source of all consumption. The business of filling it up by production and emptying it by consumption is the economic system.

So much for our first preliminary question. In the next chapter we shall inquire into the defects of the economic system. But before we do so, it is just as well to meet the objections of those who claim that, whether the system has defects or not, you will only succeed in making them worse if you start to interfere. Later on in this book there will be a brief discussion of this belief. But for the moment we do not need to make up our minds whether interference with the economic system, of any kind, is likely to make it better or worse. It is quite enough to point out that the argument is about as academic as any argument could be. In practice, the matter is decided. There is not a country in the world that is not daily interfering with the economic life of its citizens. There is not a country in the world where the number of separate interferences is not steadily increasing. There is not a country in the world where the public opinion of the citizens would allow the government to stop interfering. So if we are to have interference with the economic system, let us see that it is the most effective sort of interference. That is what this book is about. And if you want to argue about whether the best sort of interference is that which does most good or that which does least harm, go ahead and argue. But do not expect the practical world of the twentieth century to pay any attention to you.

One last preliminary hurdle. We shall be concerned in this book with the best form of economic system *for a democracy*. Just to avoid red herrings being dragged across the path later on, we had better stop to consider what we mean by democracy. Democracy has never been better defined than by Abraham Lincoln: " Government of the people, by the people, for the people." The excellence of that definition is that every word of it is essential, and if " the people " is three times repeated, it is because " the people " is three times as important as any other element in democracy. Notice that democracy is not quite the same thing as freedom. The first words of the definition are " government of the people," and there is nothing inconsonant with democracy if the people freely choose to organize themselves in a form of society that imposes restraints upon the full freedom of its individual members. But the government must be *by* the people and *for* the people. For practical purposes, that can be taken as meaning that the government must be exercised by organs freely chosen by the people, and that its only object must be to increase or safeguard the welfare of the people. There can be no dictators in a democracy ; nor must there be any attempt to elevate the state into the position of a god, to which not merely the individual citizen, but the whole body of citizens, are expected to sacrifice themselves and all they hold dear.

What has this to do with economics ? A great deal. We want to build up an economic system—

In which there is no privileged caste dictating to its subjects how they shall earn their living ;

In which the minority may have to defer to the majority, but will not be beaten, derided, or persecuted ;

In which every one will be free to organize in defence of his own interests, provided only that the welfare of the community at large is able to prevail over all sectional interests ;

In which the rights of property shall be subject to the public welfare, but the mere possession of property shall not be a capital offence or an invitation to robbery ;

In which every proposal for economic reform shall be open to free criticism and determined by the will of the community ;

In which men shall be free to think and to say what they like, and in which the guiding principles of economic reform shall be regularly submitted for approval or disapproval by the people at large, after full debate and in the presence of a free opposition.

These are matters of faith. And it is a matter of faith that they can be combined with a just and abundant economic system. If you cannot accept the faith, you had better close the book here and now, for it is in this faith that it has been written.

CHAPTER II

THE EVIL TRINITY

I

It is very customary among those who consider themselves reformers to declare that the existing economic system is breaking down. It is not. What is more, it is an unfortunate beginning to any proposals for reform to base them upon any false prediction of inevitable collapse, even though the prophecy may have the high authority of Karl Marx. Before we start abusing the economic system as it exists in Great Britain, let us first of all briefly pay tribute to its merits. It provides a higher material standard of living for the average man than has been attained in any other age or any but one or two other countries. Moreover, the standard of living shows a steady increase from decade to decade, and has lately been showing as rapid a rate of increase as at any time of which we have statistical record. Even the recurrent crises must not be exaggerated. In 1932, at the depth of the worst depression the country has ever known, almost eight out of every ten people anxious to work were in employment, and the actual production of goods and services was only about one-tenth lower than in the previous period of comparatively high activity.

There is thus quite a lot to be said for the present system. What that means in practice is that an alternative system will have to be very good if it is to be better. Those who argue that the existing system is so bad that any alternative would be preferable are merely deceiving themselves and their disciples. Let us be quite clear about that. But let us be equally clear that there are grave defects in the existing system. This book could easily be devoted merely to a catalogue of them. But in the main they can be generalized under three heads.

In the first place, the pool that constitutes the national income is not large enough. The amount of goods and services available for the consumption of the community is not enough to ensure a decent living to every individual. We could do with vastly more goods and services out of the pool, which means that we must find ways of putting vastly more goods and services into it.

Secondly, the distribution of the goods and services in the pool is shockingly unequal. Some people derive from it as many of the material good things of life as anybody in their wildest dreams could imagine ; others derive only the barest minimum necessary to keep body and soul together. Whatever may be the inequalities of the contributions made to the pool by different individuals, they cannot be as unequal as this.

Thirdly, the size of the pool varies greatly from time to time. There are some years in which the value of goods and services contributed to the pool, and, consequently, the amount that can be drawn out, is large and increasing. There are other years when part of the community stands idle, with the result that the goods and services available to be drawn out of the pool are even more insufficient than at other times.

These, then, are the three great defects of the economic system :

Poverty
Inequality
Irregularity.

It will be worth while to examine each of them in turn.

2

In any criticism of the economic system poverty must be placed first. Even if a pool of the national income could be divided with absolute equality between the individuals who compose the community, so that each one had exactly the same income as every other one, there would not be enough to guarantee a full and adequate living to each. The approximate magnitude of the sums involved can easily be ascertained. After setting aside the necessary provision for maintaining and increasing the productive equipment of the community, the national income would barely be enough, even in the best year we have ever known, to provide an income of 35s. a week for each individual. Now there are many thousands of families who would be only too glad to receive 35s. a week for every member of the family. A husband and wife and one child on this calculation would receive something like £5. 5s. a week, which would be riches for most working-class families. But 35s. a week per head is not sufficient to provide for every member of the community all the material benefits that are at present enjoyed by the well-to-do ; it is not nearly enough to provide what the middle-classes regard as necessities ; it is not enough to ensure really attractive housing, adequate food, warm clothing, travel, recreation, entertainment, and the other good things to which modern man aspires. To take only the primary necessity of food, it has been calculated that the community needs to increase its consumption of food by between one-eighth and one-quarter. And even this figure of 35s. a week is attainable only with low unemployment and an absolutely equal division of the national income. No community yet has found means for assuring that both these assumptions can be made at once, or even either separately. Moreover, Great Britain, of which we have been speaking, is among the very richest of the nations of the earth. It is quite exceptional to be able to approach even as closely as this to the ideal of a sufficiency for all. In practical conditions it must be recognized that there is poverty in the world, not only because of the unequal distribution of wealth, but also because of the insufficient volume of goods and services which is produced.

It is the fashion in some quarters to proclaim that the problem of production is solved. It is claimed that we have now reached the stage in human history at which we can produce enough of the material things of life to provide for all our citizens. Unfortunately, any such statement is entirely untrue. Those who make it are not so foolish as to pretend that everybody already has all that he wants ; they maintain merely that the economic system *could*, if its managers chose, produce enough for all. A variety of arguments is used in support of this thesis. Its advocates usually make great play with a number of examples that can be quoted of useful goods being actually destroyed because of the insufficient price that can be obtained for them. Coffee, as is well known, has been burned in Brazil to prevent it coming on to the world market ; fish has been thrown back into the sea because it could not be sold at a remunerative price ; wheat has been fed to cattle because insufficient could be got for it to pay the costs of transport to the human market. But these occurrences, though they naturally excite a great deal of attention, are exceptions to the rule. Far and away the vast majority of goods produced are consumed. The believers in the " age of plenty " are on much sounder ground when they argue that although everything that is produced is consumed, less is produced than could be. This is unquestionably true ; but it is important to be clear in our minds in what quantitative degree it is true. It is said that if all the mechanical devices of the inventor were fully exploited, production of goods would be greatly speeded up ; but it is important to know *how much* they would be speeded up. It is claimed that the operation of the monetary system prevents the production of goods from reaching the dimensions that it might. It is argued that the private ownership of capital restricts production. It is a comparatively easy matter, however, to see how much truth there can be in all these assertions.

The most obvious scope for increased production of goods and services would lie in the employment of those who are now out of work. We know how many of these there are. At the moment this book is being written the number of insured workpeople in Great Britain who are out of work is about 12 per cent. of the total. That means that the present production of goods and services is being effected by only 88 per cent. of the population available for work. If the remaining 12 per cent. could be put to work, the total production of the community should increase in the proportion of 88 : 100, or roughly, by one-seventh. Now, of course, this is a very sweeping assumption, since there has never been a time in the history of any community when there has been no un-employment at all. At any one time there are certain people who are out of work, if only because they are passing from one job to another. In any changing, dynamic community there are some occupations that are declining and some others that are expanding, and the process of transferring labour from one class to the other cannot be carried out instantaneously. Moreover, there are in any community a number of people who are unemployable because of personal defects of physique or character. Let us, however, for the moment forget all these very necessary qualifications, and assume that every last man and woman in the ranks of the un-employed could be re-absorbed. The production of goods and services, which is another way of saying the income available for the consumption of the community, would be increased by about one-seventh.

Anybody who asserts that production could be in-creased by a larger proportion than this is talking sense only if he can prove that there are methods already in existence by which the number of goods and services produced in a day by the average man could be increased. Most people who make this assertion are deluded by a few striking inventions in a very few industries. We have all of us, for example, heard of the miraculous glass-bottle machines, by which one man can make a hundred times the number of bottles that it formerly took twenty men to blow, or of the brick-making machines which can similarly increase the efficiency of that industry. But what is usually forgotten is that such examples not only *are* not typical of the whole range of production, but *could* not be typical. If you examine these stories, you will find that every one of them relates to new methods of making things. Now, in a modern community such as Great Britain only about a third of all the occupied people earn their livings by making things ; the rest of us make our livings by selling or transporting goods, or by rendering services of all kinds. Before you can prove that there are ways of increasing the total production of the community, you must prove that they are ways that will increase the production not merely of the factory worker, but of the shop assistant, the tram conductor, the book-keeper, the journalist, and a great variety of other similar occupations. It needs only a moment's reflection to see that there is no such magical formula. Everybody who writes or lectures on economic matters is familiar with the economic sectary who roundly asserts that if only the system were changed the volume of production could be doubled overnight. I wonder if these people realize exactly what they are asserting. They are, in fact, claiming that they know of some means by which the shop assistant can serve twice as many customers in the day, by which the ticket collector can collect twice as many fares, by which the tram driver can drive twice as many passengers, by which the journalist can write twice as many articles, and by which the lorry driver can drive twice as many miles. These are the occupations that are typical of a modern community—far more typical than the worker who makes things in a factory.

The truth is that under any conceivable system, with any conceivable monetary arrangements, the total volume of production of the community, which is just the same thing as the total volume of its consumption, could not possibly be increased immediately, or even within a short time, by anything like the proportions that are so facilely bandied about in the conversation of many people who have never stopped to think what their words mean. The most efficient imaginable system of organization, which performed the miracle not only of finding a job instantaneously for every one of a score of millions of individuals, but also ensured that every improved method of producing wealth was no sooner invented than it was universally applied, could not, at the present moment, produce a national income any larger, at the very most, than a quarter bigger than the present national income. Even that figure depends upon the most outrageously impossible assumptions.

It may very well be that some reform of the economic system will enable us to increase the production and consumption of goods and services more rapidly than they are at present increasing. That is a question that will have to be examined later in this book. But for the moment it is hardly relevant. What we are establishing at the moment is merely that there is still plenty of room for increase in the national income. It is not yet nearly large enough, and no change of system could instantaneously increase it by a sufficient amount. To state this truth is frequently to be accused of pessimism. But there is no pessimism in it except such as emerges from the facts. Why should it be considered an example of economic defeatism to declare that the world does not yet produce enough material goods to supply the needs of its human inhabitants ? It is manifestly true that there *was* an insufficiency—that there could not, even with perfect organization, have been a sufficiency—in days gone by. Why should it suddenly have become untrue to-day, merely because it is we and not our ancestors who are alive? Admittedly, it is an unpleasant fact that the world cannot create enough. If you wish, it is disagreeable, even scandalous. But that does not make it any less true. And the proper conclusion is surely not to abuse the system for failing to do what no system could do, but rather to press on as rapidly as possible with the increase in the national income and to examine what amendments of the system will best contribute to that end.

The first requirement of the ideal economic system is, then, that it must be *efficient* in the production of goods and services. Efficiency in this sense is something rather different from technical efficiency. An industry may be very smart and chromium-plated, and do everything with the latest appliances, and yet be economically inefficient. The most efficient economic system is that which produces the greatest volume of useful goods and services with the least expenditure of human effort. The most efficient industry is, broadly speaking, that which charges least for its products—in other words, that which demands the lowest tribute in other forms of human effort in return for the particular varieties of human effort embodied in the goods it produces. We are closer in our generation and in our country to a solution of the problem of production than any previous age or most other countries. But we have not got there yet. For at least one more generation, and perhaps two, one of the first essentials of economic policy must be to see that the sum total of goods and services available each year for consumption is at least well maintained, and, if possible, rapidly increased. Those who claim that the problem of production is solved are in truth obstructing the attainment of what they desire, for, as we shall see in a later chapter, the very widespread acceptance of the fallacy that there is already a sufficiency of goods and services in existence for all to enjoy an adequate income is being used in many countries as the basis of policies which are in effect increasing the already insupportable degree of poverty.

Every suggested economic policy should, therefore, be closely examined to see whether or not it would increase the volume of goods and services being placed in the national pool. This does not mean that there is never a case for the temporary restriction of production in some particular industry ; in a later chapter we shall have to examine the circumstances in which such restriction is permissible, but here we are concerned with the main principle that the restriction or limitation of production must be an exceptional and emergency device. In general the chief aim of economic policy must be to expand the production of goods and services as rapidly as possible.

3

The second great defect of our economic system is the inequality of incomes which it permits to exist between different members of the same community. The facts about this inequality are not often realized in their astonishing magnitude. We can divide the people of Great Britain very broadly into three classes according to their incomes. The lowest class of incomes consists of those of less than £5 a week. The rich may be defined as those who have to pay surtax, *i.e.* whose incomes are more than £2,000 a year. The middle class are those in between. If we are talking about the number of *people*, the poor on this definition make up 90 per cent. of the whole, but they draw only just over half of the *income*. The rich are only half of 1 per cent. of the people in the country, but they have one-sixth of the income. The middle class are one-tenth of the people, but they have between one-quarter and one-third of the income. The same facts can be put in another striking way. A fair average figure for the wages of an adult male wage-earner in Great Britain is 65s. a week, or £169 a year. But there are in this country something like five hundred people who have incomes of £169 a *day*. It is quite impossible to exaggerate the enormous difference in wealth and welfare between the rich and the poor.

There can be no doubt about the main cause of this striking degree of inequality in the distribution of wealth. It comes from the ownership of property. The ownership of property is not the sole cause. There are differences, it is true, in the value to the community of the work done by different individuals ; the work done by the surgeon who carries out a difficult major operation is clearly much more valuable than that of the charwoman who cleans up afterwards, and their services are rightly very differently rewarded. Further than that, the rewards paid for different sorts of work are frequently out of all proportion to the relative value of the services, as when the movie star earns in a day as much as the slum clergyman in a year, although the good they do to their fellow-men may not be so very different. But if these differences in the value of services rendered, or in the rewards that are given for different kinds of services, were the only inequalities in existence, we could forget about them. There would still be a few men and women earning very large incomes owing to the rarity of their professional gifts, but the degree of inequality to which they would give rise would be so small as not to be worth worrying about. Much the larger and most damaging degree of inequality arises because the ownership of property is very unequally distributed. Approximately one-third of the total national income is the income of property, and, though very many people have some tiny share in the income of property, the bulk of it flows only into a few hands. Four-fifths of British property is owned by one-twentieth of the adults in the country ; over half the property is owned by less than one-hundredth of the people. Far and away the vast majority of people, including most of those who earn substantial salaries, have no income, or only a small income, from interest or dividends. The rich, broadly speaking, are the owners of property, and the owners of property are the rich. They have indeed a double advantage, for in the present organization of society the ownership of property makes it considerably easier to obtain a well-remunerated salaried job. If you are a large shareholder in a company you stand a very much better chance of becoming its managing-director than if you merely rely upon your abilities. Many of the large salaries must, therefore, be regarded as the indirect result of property-owning.

To say that the inequality of wealth arises from the ownership of property, however, is only half the truth ; the real answer is that it is due to the inheritance of property. A few individuals manage to accumulate enormous fortunes within their own lifetime, but these again are exceptions rather than the rule. We could safely allow the present inequality of salaries, and we could also allow any man to draw income from the property he had himself acquired, and we should still be faced with only a comparatively minor degree of inequality. What causes the continuing schism of society between rich and poor is the fact that rich men can hand on their wealth to their sons. The rich man's son already has an advantage, since his father can give him an education which is either technically better than that which the poor man's son receives or, at least, takes place at the right sort of school for giving him a privileged claim on the high-salaried positions. If, in addition to the cash advantages of public school and university, the rich man's son inherits an income for which he does not need to work, he is put on the path of life with a very substantial advantage over his competitors. It would be an interesting exercise, if it were possible, to go through the list of people whose incomes at present exceed £5,000 per annum, and to discover what proportion of them owe that income wholly or mainly to their own efforts, and what proportion have merely inherited it, or the chance of making it, from their forefathers. No one can know the answer, but it would be very surprising if the proportion of those who really earn their wealth were more than a tenth, or at most, a fifth, of the total.

This inequality of opportunities is a fundamental evil in itself. It is wrong that some should go through life with every conceivable material advantage, while others should be subjected at every turn to the cumulative penalties of the under-privileged. Not everybody, perhaps, would be found to agree with the last sentence, but whatever one's views on the morals of the matter, it is at any rate true that such inequality is inconsistent with a really free and equal society. It is not merely that the rich get their way so easily and so disproportionately to their numbers. In many of the things of life they get their way merely by buying it, and even when it comes to an open and conscious conflict between the interests of the rich and poor, the rich are in a very strong position because of the fact that their income does not need continually repeated effort to bring it in. Unlike the poor, they do not starve when they go on strike. In innumerable ways, in our present society, the dice are loaded in favour of the rich. But democracy cannot be fairly played with loaded dice.

For all these false values and unworthy distinctions the unequal distribution of property is fundamentally to blame. No country can be a true democracy if it allows great inequalities of wealth and rank, except such as are based on differences of worth. What is more, no country that is ruled by universal suffrage can fail to aspire, however spasmodically, to a removal of these differences.

This is the argument against inequality on the moral and political plane. But it is possible to add economic arguments also. Inequality leads to great economic waste. The most flagrant example of this fact is the wasteful and utterly useless forms which expenditure takes at the upper end of the social scale in the effort to keep up with fashion or to outshine one's slightly less wealthy neighbours. But the wastes are really greater at the other end of the scale. A community that allows its poorest families to live at the starvation line is not doing what it should in its own interests to maintain the value of its human capital. The full force of this can be seen on any occasion when groups of rich and poor can be compared. The average height of schoolboys of the same age, for example, is several inches more at the boarding-schools to which the rich send their sons than at the board schools to which the poor send their sons. It has similarly been pointed out that the contrast in stature between Labour and Conservative Members of Parliament can be clearly seen in the division lobbies of the House of Commons. Stature, of course, is not everything, and he who adds a cubit to his stature is not necessarily better equipped for taking thought; but, other things being equal, under-nourishment of the body is likely to be accompanied by under-nourishment of the mind. Poverty, as we have seen, would not be abolished even if there were complete equality of income, but it would be very much less, and part at least of the consequences of poverty can readily be set in the score against inequality.

There is another way in which the inequality of incomes causes economic waste to the community. It has already been pointed out that it is much easier for a property-owner to put himself into a highly remunerated position. But the highly remunerated positions are, by and large, those whose exercise is most crucial for the proper organization of the community. It only needs a slight acquaintance with, for example, the City of London to realize how many of the crucially important administrative posts go to men whose only qualification is the inheritance of wealth. In firm after firm the rich man holds the power, and is served by others whose competence is far greater. It is true that the dominant position in our present system of the property-owner enables the exceptionally able business man to control great aggregations of capital, which is an advantage for the productivity and efficiency of the system. But it also puts the same control in the hands of his sons and his grandsons, who may be—but are probably not—the ideal persons to exercise it. On balance, a community which selected all its leaders by merit could have better leadership of its economic affairs. Inequality of wealth almost certainly reduces the efficiency of management.

Income from inherited property must, then, be looked upon as the chief cause of inequality and of the many disadvantages that flow from it. Income from property usually takes the form of profits and interest. But because the inequality of wealth arises from profits and interest it would not be right to suggest, as is frequently argued, that the cure for inequality is to abolish profits and interest. The objection is not to the fact that there are such things as profits and interest, but firstly, to the fact that they are concentrated in a few hands; and secondly, to the excessive economic power and political privilege which their ownership confers. The object of reform should not be the large amount of money going in profits and interest, but the small number of pockets into which it goes. This may seem to be a quibbling point, but it is really of outstanding importance, for, as we shall see in a later chapter, social reformers have often got into difficulties because, in attacking the privileges of the profit-owners, they have really attacked profits, and seriously deranged the working of the economic mechanism. This is not the place to develop this particular argument in detail; the only point with which we are concerned at the moment is to notice that it is not the institution of property, but its unequal distribution, which in turn is largely due to the institution of inheritance, that is responsible for the shocking degree of inequality.

Before leaving the subject of inequality it is as well to answer the objection that one sometimes hears, that it is already in process of abolition by means of heavy taxation. At first sight it might seem so. Income tax, together with surtax, takes more than half of the largest incomes, and the rates of death duties on the biggest estates are very onerous. But it needs only a glance at the available figures to realize that even these heavy rates of taxation have done very little to reduce the amount of inequality. We have had them now in this country for twenty years, but there are more people to-day with incomes of £8,000 a year than there were with incomes of £5,000 a year before the heavy taxation was imposed. And although in twenty years roughly two-thirds of the family fortunes of the country must have been subject to death duties, there is an increase rather than a diminution in the number of millionaires dying each year. The heavy taxation was imposed with the object not of diminishing inequality, but of raising revenue, and it seems to have succeeded exactly in its intentions. Taxation provides no alibi; we cannot conveniently assume that we need only maintain the present burden of taxation for inequality slowly to fade away. It needs further and more active steps, which must be put high on the agenda of reform.

4

The third great defect of the existing economic system is much the most puzzling of the three. With the other two—poverty and inequality—it is an easy matter to identify the chief cause. It may be hard to remedy it, but at least it is possible to state in dogmatic terms what should be the objective of policy. But this is not so with the ups and downs of trade, which we have listed as the third great evil. If this book had been written thirty years ago it is questionable whether the irregularity of the economic system would have been admitted to equality as a major defect. But since the war of 1914–18 we have learned through bitter experience that the irregularity of trade and the unemployment to which it gives rise are one of the chief dangers facing the world. I say "we have learned," because there has been a definite change of opinion in the public mind on the matter, a change of opinion which has not yet, perhaps, had the consequences upon economic thinking which logically follow from it. Thirty years ago, if you had stopped a man in the street and asked him what, in his opinion, should be the chief aim of economic policy, he would almost certainly have replied that it was to remove poverty. Or if he had some acquaintance with economic terminology he would have said that it was to increase productivity and raise the average real income per head of the community. The whole of the accepted body of classical economics is based upon that assumption. But if you stopped a man in the street to-day and asked him the same question, he would certainly answer that the aim of economic policy should be to remove unemployment.

This is more than a merely verbal distinction; it represents a real difference. It is not very difficult to prove that the average real income per head of the wage-earners of Great Britain was at least as great in the depression year 1932 as in the relatively prosperous year 1929, or even greater. The great world depression which came between these two dates had the double effect of increasing unemployment and reducing the prices of food and other necessities. Those who remained in work benefited very largely from the fall in prices, which was very much greater than the fall in wage-rates, and, in purely economic terms, the gain to them was larger than the loss of consuming power by the unemployed. If the economic welfare of a country is measured solely by the quantity of goods it consumes, then the British community probably, and the British working class certainly, was enjoying greater welfare in 1932 than in 1929. But this comparison merely exposes the inadequacy of any such definition of economic welfare. Unemployment, indeed, imposes a special variety of inequality of income, an inequality, not between the rich and the poor, but between the employed and the unemployed. And even though the grand total of real income may rise, if it is accompanied by growing inequality of distribution the ordinary man will conclude that it is a diminution rather than an increase of welfare. And the ordinary man will be quite right.

We must, therefore, as a result of the last two decades, place the problem of economic fluctuations high on our list of defects to be cured. It must be obvious that the problem of economic fluctuations, or the trade cycle— by which name the phenomenon is generally known— cannot be fully discussed here. It has been responsible for more weighty tomes in the last few years than any other economic problem, and even so, it is questionable how far there is agreement among economists as to its nature and cause. It will therefore not be possible in these pages to do more than sketch very briefly some of the chief explanations that are offered for the existence of the

trade cycle. These explanations are not alternative so
much as complementary. Only the cranks maintain that
there is one single cause of the trade cycle, and the differences between more responsible writers are very largely
differences of emphasis.

The most familiar explanation of the trade cycle
relates it to the volume of money in existence. This
theory has many detailed forms, but in general all of
them maintain that fluctuations are caused by the supply
of money being either too large or too small to fit the
economic circumstances of the moment. More precisely, most of these theories urge that a depression occurs
when, after a period of too abundant supply of money,
the supply is suddenly restricted. But for our present
purpose we need not follow this doctrine into its recesses
of refinement. It is sufficient to point out that it ascribes
the trade cycle to a maladjustment between the quantity
of money in existence and the need for it.

Another group of theories connects the trade cycle
with fluctuations in agriculture. Agriculture is still by far
the world's largest industry, and it is the one where the
volume of production from year to year is least under the
control of man. It is never possible, except within a very
wide margin of error, to predict what next year's crop
will be. If the crop is excessively large, the ensuing glut
may force prices so low as to ruin the agricultural
community. In economic terms, this means that in that
particular year the world is devoting too many of its
resources of capital and labour to growing agricultural
crops. It is an excess not in the sense that the additional
food would not gladly be eaten by the poor, but in the
sense that the production of some commodities other
than food would have yielded a greater return of wealth

(*e.g.* the poor might have preferred more clothes or better houses). If the crop is short, the opposite consequences follow. Prices are driven to very high levels, and the world finds itself for a year in the position of devoting fewer of its resources to agriculture than on a balanced consideration would pay it. Once again we need not delay to trace out the manifold consequences of either state of affairs. In the one case the farmers' income is unduly low, and their purchasing power correspondingly affected. In the other case the industrial workers suffer from a loss of real income ; they have to pay more for their food, and consequently have less resources available for purchasing industrial commodities of all sorts. In either case, however, there is a maladjustment in the distribution of available resources between agriculture and industry.

Another school of economists finds the main explanation of the trade cycle in the alternations of public psychology. This means a bit more than merely that the public feels optimistic at one period and pessimistic at another—though there is a great deal of substance even in that simple explanation. The more refined version of the theory does, indeed, postulate that there are alternations of optimism and pessimism, but it refers in particular to the attitude of business men towards investment in the fixed capital of their businesses. In one period, the managers of business, having experienced that the demand for their products has been steadily rising for some years, begin to feel confident that it will continue to rise, and they go ahead with the necessary arrangements to build factories, to make machinery, and to recruit the labour for providing the increased supply of goods for which they anticipate a demand. The expenditure of this money on capital equipment reinforces the wave of prosperity, and it is part of the theory that business men tend to feel optimistic in this way at the same time, so that all industries undertake an extension of their capital equipment at the same moment. When this capital equipment comes into production, however, it is discovered that too much of it has been provided, and that the quantity of goods that can now be produced by these industries is larger than the demand for them. Indeed, the cessation of building and equipment and the dismissal of the men who have been engaged upon them tends to reduce the demand which the buildings and the machinery were designed to meet. Disappointment over the results of these capital extensions leads to a second period in which there is less provision of capital equipment than usual, and a consequent depression. This theory, then, finds the explanation in a maladjustment between business men's estimates of the quantity of goods that will be demanded and the actual demand.

In recent years there has been a strong tendency among economists to find the main explanation of the trade cycle in an extension of the theory which was very briefly and superficially expounded in the last paragraph. It will therefore be worth our while to inquire into it a little more closely.

Every occupied person has an income. Out of that income he provides for his own requirements and those of the people dependent upon him. His consumption may be exactly the same as his income. It cannot for an indefinite length of time be larger. But it may be smaller, and the balance between consumption and income is saving. The saving of a nation is, of course, the aggregate of the saving of all the individuals composing the nation. It represents the difference between the value of the economic services rendered by the members of the community and the value of the consumption goods used up—the difference between the value of what is put into the pool and what is drawn out for consumption. This saving can be thought of for the moment as a sum of money put aside to increase the capital of the nation.

Just as the income of an individual or a nation is divided between consumption and saving, so the production of a community consists of some goods for immediate consumption and some capital goods—that is, goods which will assist consumption at some later date, either because, like machinery, they assist in the more plentiful production of consumption goods, or else because, like houses, they are goods which will serve the consumer for many years to come.

Thus income is divided into consumption and savings, and production into consumption goods and capital goods. Now clearly, if the economic system is working smoothly, the money devoted to consumption will exactly purchase the consumption goods, and the money devoted to saving will exactly purchase the capital goods. But there is nothing to ensure that the two categories will exactly coincide at any one moment. Those who do the saving are not, by and large, those who decide to make the capital goods. If business men decide to make more capital goods than there are savings to pay for, that means that the volume of production of capital goods is larger than can be permanently maintained. Men will be drawn into the industries that make capital goods, and then after a period will find that there is no work for them to do. If, on the other hand, the volume of production of capital goods is smaller than would be justified

by the current volume of savings, there will be unemployment in the capital goods industries. It is
probable also that the demand for consumption goods
will be less than the supply of them, with the result of
falling prices and unemployment in those industries also.

This is a highly simplified description of the theory,
which is calculated to make the experts shudder with
horror at the absence of qualifications and refinements.
But for our present purpose it is quite enough to say that
this currently accepted theory of the trade cycle finds the
explanation in a maladjustment between the volume of
savings and the volume of production of capital goods—
in short, in a maladjustment between the demand for
and supply of capital.

All these four explanations of the trade cycle thus find
the cause in some form of maladjustment. They each
maintain that the trade cycle is caused by the economic
system of the world finding itself in a false position—a
position, that is, different from what it would have been
if all the facts had been known and the decisions taken on
the basis of them. The trade cycle can thus be said with
some degree of confidence to be due to some part of the
economic system failing to perform its proper function.

The trade cycle is usually a matter of a few years only.
Periods of relative prosperity or relative depression rarely
last as long as, and never longer than, five years. But
mixed with these cyclical maladjustments there are, of
course, others of longer history. The long decline of
older methods of road transport before the advance of
the railway a hundred years ago, for example, lasted
more than a few years. In our own times the causes that
have led to the chronic depression of the coal and cotton
industries have outlasted a single trade cycle. We

must not, therefore, allow ourselves to slip into the belief that the only maladjustments in the system are those that give rise to the trade cycle. But there can be little doubt that the trade cycle is very largely due to a particular variety of economic maladjustments.

Some of these maladjustments might be prevented by a wise and far-seeing policy. This is particularly true of the maladjustments that arise from either a super-abundance or a shortage of money, and there are many who consequently preach the virtues of a conscious manipulation of money for the purpose of ironing-out the trade cycle. But most of the maladjustments are not preventable. Nothing that man has yet discovered can remove the possibility of bumper crops ; we have not yet discovered how to make business men immune to the alternating temptations to over-estimate and under-estimate the prospects of their businesses ; we have not yet discovered means of adjusting the volume of production of capital goods with precision to the volume of savings. As for the maladjustments that come about when coachmakers are ruined by the advent of railways, or coal miners by the development of hydro-electric power, so far from being able to prevent them, it is very doubtful whether we should want to prevent them, if we could, since all economic progress depends upon these adjustments being made.

But if the emergence of maladjustments cannot be avoided, it is possible to aim at speeding up the process by which the economic system adapts itself to changing circumstances. Lord Keynes, in a striking metaphor, once remarked that many of the mistakes of economic policy arise from the fact that we apply the theory of liquids to what is a viscous mass. We cannot possibly, even if we should wish to, petrify the economic system in its present shape ; we cannot legislate that for all time exactly the same proportion of the people's consumption shall be devoted to the purchase of different commodities as at present. But that would be the only means of ensuring that there was never any need to make painful transfer of resources of labour and capital from one employment to another. Since, then, the theory of liquids must continue to apply, we must endeavour to reduce the viscosity of the economic system.

There is good reason for believing that the greater intensity of the trade cycle in recent years has been due to the fact that the adaptability of the economic system has been diminished. This is, in part, a natural tendency, which can be connected with the fact that our population is no longer rapidly increasing. Some of the decline in the system's adaptability, however, is by an unfortunate paradox the direct result of the need for adjustment. Adjustment inevitably means that people are being forced to change their habits and their employments, to abandon the security they have built up for themselves, whether as workers or as employers, and to embark on fresh ventures. Naturally the process is fiercely resented and stubbornly resisted, and the first instinct of an industry or a community threatened by such change is to organize to prevent it. It does not need much imagination to see that this inevitably slows down the necessary process of adjustment. Faced with the need for liquidity, the organizations both of capital and of labour are in many respects taking action that is calculated to increase the viscosity of the economic system. Moreover, the institution of social services increases the ability of men to say that they will not abandon the industries in which they have hitherto been employed, but will rather live upon resources provided by the community. Social services are usually thought of as providing for the needs of the worker alone, but in recent years in Great Britain there has been a great increase in the number of doles for capital—subsidies offered to this industry and that to enable it to resist the pressure for change. We must learn that giving aid to those who suffer through the process of change is one thing, but that encouraging them to obstruct the changes by which progress moves is another.

While the adaptability of the economic system has thus been falling, the need for it has been increasing. It is obvious that in proportion as an economic system grows complex, the chances of maladjustment increase. This is particularly so with a system which uses a large amount of fixed capital equipment, for in that case the decisions which determine the volume of production have to be made a long time before the production goes on the market to be consumed, and the chances of mistakes are correspondingly increased.

It is not merely the growth in the complexity of the economic system which increases the opportunities for maladjustment, but the growth in the income which it provides for the individual citizen has the same effect. When the economic system is so poverty-stricken that the vast majority of mankind contrive to have only the barest minimum of food, clothing, and shelter, there is no room for many fluctuations in demand. But as soon as it becomes possible for the mass of the people to enjoy any luxuries or semi-luxuries, much greater opportunities for fluctuation begin to appear. The greater the margin above the subsistence level, the more there is that can, in case of necessity, be done without. Even apart from that, where things are not absolute necessities, there is clearly a much greater field for the fickleness of taste and fashion to play its part. It is an observed and rather ominous fact that, on the whole, the richest countries have the deepest depressions.

Finally, we must list, as a factor tending to increase the likelihood of maladjustments, the tendency which has materialized in recent years for countries to make themselves as far as possible self-sufficient within their own borders. This is not the place to examine the causes of this tendency, or even to argue its rights and wrongs. But it is clear that the smaller the area within which adjustments are allowed to be made by the normal process of interchange between nations, the larger is the likelihood of serious maladjustments appearing. A crop failure in one country, for example, is of no importance if the resources of the rest of the world can be drawn upon. But if foreign food is kept out by high tariffs or prohibitions, the small crop failure becomes of immediate importance. And what is so clearly true of agriculture is in the same sense true of industry. A world divided into a number of small water-tight compartments is likely to be not only a poorer but also a less flexible world than one which encourages trade between its members.

The warning given at the beginning of this section had better be repeated. This is not in the least intended as a full description of the trade cycle. It is intended merely to support the point that since the fluctuations of trade are one of the major defects of the economic system, and since these fluctuations can be ascribed to the difficulty with which the system adjusts itself to changing circumstances, the increase in the flexibility of the system must be put alongside the increase of its efficiency and the increase of its equity as one of the three great aims of economic policy.

5

These, then, are the evil trinity of defects in the present economic system—poverty, which denotes an inadequate production of wealth, the inequality of its distribution, and the irregularity with which it fluctuates from year to year.

We have also, in the course of the discussion of these three defects, detected in each case the necessary antidote to the poison. To get rid of poverty we need an economic system that can produce more wealth out of each day's work of the average man : in a word, we need a more efficient system. To abolish the corrupting scandal of the material rewards of life being out of all proportion to the differences of personal contributions to the social income, we need a more equal distribution of property ; in a word, a more equitable system. And finally, to prevent the disturbing fluctuations of prosperity, which remove all security from economic life, we need a system that adjusts itself more freely to the changing needs of man and to the changing bounty of Nature : in a word, a more adaptable system.

Political democracy, in its modern form, goes back to the men of the French Revolution with their triple watchword of "Liberty, Equality, Fraternity." Economic democracy needs a similar watchword— "Efficiency, Equity, Adaptability."

CHAPTER III

DEMOCRATIC CREDO

THIS chapter brings together into four propositions the essential elements of a democratic economy. In part it is a recapitulation of what has gone before, in part it draws a few of the inferences that are necessary before we can proceed with the consideration of a system of democratic economy.

I

The first proposition needs no further discussion, since it has formed the substance of the last chapter. The aim of the democratic economy must be to reduce poverty, inequality, and irregularity, and its methods of doing so must be to foster efficiency, equity, and adaptability.

2

No one of the three objectives can safely be given preference over the other two.

This is a view that would not commend itself to everybody ; indeed there are large sections of opinion which habitually concentrate upon one of the three essential elements. Those who have most at heart the plight of the poor, especially those who represent them in Parliament, concentrate upon the need for a more equal distribution of wealth almost to the exclusion of everything else. They are concerned with getting for the poor a larger slice of the cake. On cross-examination they would not deny the importance of increasing, or at least not diminishing, the size of the whole cake. But in practice, many of their policies seem to forget about the whole cake in concentrating on the slice. On the other hand, from those whose business in life is to organize and manage the great industries, we naturally hear much more about the importance of maintaining and increasing the efficiency of industry. They would not deny, when questioned, the necessity of securing a fair deal for the workers ; but in practice the maintenance of industrial efficiency is a more important thing to them than the increase in the standard of living of their employees.

In spite of these firm preferences, however, I do not think that any observer who is both comparatively unprejudiced and comparatively well-informed about the nature of the economic system could justifiably conclude that any one of our three objectives is preferable to the others. Suppose, for example, that we choose equity, and decide so to organize our programme of reform that the inequality of wealth is rapidly reduced, even at the cost of some reduction in production and some reduction in the elasticity with which the system can adjust itself to change. There are many people who deliberately advocate such a course, but it is not one which would in practice commend itself to the public. For one thing, even the ideal of equality becomes less attractive when it is interpreted as a dead level of poverty for all. And for another thing, a change by which the gainers gained very little, while the losers lost very much would be highly unpopular; such experiments cannot be tried with impunity in a democratic state. We must never forget, in our aspirations for equality, that there is only one way of abolishing poverty, and that is by an increase in the efficiency of the economic machine. Increased production will abolish poverty more quickly if it is accompanied by increased equality of distribution. But the two must march together, and neither one will be fully effective without the other.

Adaptability has fewer vocal friends than either efficiency or equity. Neither the ranks of organized labour nor those of capital appear as its champions; indeed, as we shall see in the next two chapters, many of those tendencies of the present world that can be traced back to the insistence of one side or the other have the effect of substantially reducing the elasticity of the economic system. But it must be apparent to anybody who has followed the argument of the previous chapter that adaptability does not yield in the slightest degree to the other two as an essential need of a modern community. Just because the claims of efficiency and equity are vociferous and familiar, it is peculiarly essential to emphasize those of adaptability. Of what avail are increases in the efficiency of the economic machine or in the equality with which its rewards are distributed, if both are periodically to be lost in catastrophic depressions of trade, with their consequences, at the best, of panic policies, and at the worst, of savage revolutions? Moreover, the need for adaptability is rising. The twentieth century, in comparison with the nineteenth, will not be a period of rapid expansion. Geographically the world is occupied; its natural resources are already known, and in many cases already exploited. In country after country the increase of the population is coming to an end, and a slow decline is about to begin. The task of the economic mechanism in the future will not be so much to expand to meet ever-increasing opportunities and demands, but rather continuously to rearrange the disposition of resources in order to meet the slow change in the requirements of the population whose total numbers are stable. In these circumstances, the need for adaptability is rapidly increasing. No economic policy in this century which fails to make the fullest allowance for maintaining and increasing the suppleness of economic organization will stand a chance of being successful.

No one of the three elements can thus be ignored, or even preferred above the others. Fortunately, however, they are not exclusive opposites ; the pursuit of one does not necessarily imply the worsening of the other two. Sometimes, it is true, it is necessary to sacrifice a little of one for a great gain in the other two, but in general it is fully possible to serve all three. Such at least has been the experience of the last hundred years, when there has been a very considerable increase in efficiency with some diminution of inequality, and, at least until the last two decades, no very noticeable decrease in adaptability. This last of the three has, indeed, become rather a Cinderella in the world since 1918 ; but such a tendency is not inevitable, and once its importance is realized there is no reason to believe that the community cannot provide for it as it has begun to provide for equality. Efficiency, Equity, and Adaptability can march together.

3

The third essential principle can best be put in the words of a parable. We must rebuild the station while the trains are running. The most obvious meaning of this is that we must eschew all revolutionary methods, which would produce a catastrophe in order to free the ground for rebuilding. Such methods have never yet succeeded in increasing the net total of welfare. It is so much more difficult to rebuild after a catastrophe than to bring the existing structure down, and in the meantime a formidable total of misery is piled up, larger than can ever be offset by the better world which slowly rises from the ruins. But the principle stated in the parable goes rather beyond the mere avoidance of revolutionary action. It means that in all schemes of reform the greatest care must be taken to see that the system is reformed as a going concern. We cannot stop for repairs, and even on a plane far lower than catastrophe or revolution, every hesitation in the smooth running of the economic system means less food for some one. And since those who advocate drastic measures are usually the champions of the poor, it is a sobering reflection to bear in mind that it is always the poor who suffer first, last, and most seriously from any interference with the daily operation of the economic machine.

Another aspect of the same matter is that we cannot afford to look too far ahead. One of the defects of *laisser-faire* economics was that it was inclined to advocate policies which did not produce their results for several generations. It was altogether too fond of long-run considerations, although in the long run, as Lord Keynes has said, we are all dead. No community, of course, will survive unless it takes some thought for the future, but policies which concentrate too much on the distant future are a snare and a delusion. Not only is there the difficulty of accurately predicting the circumstances of the future, but there is the danger of very considerably under-estimating the sacrifices that the present will have to make for the glory of the future. Russia, for example, went through five years of bloodshed and five years of privation in order to assure herself a brighter future. Was it worth while to the generation of Russians who went through it? We have a clear duty to posterity, which can be set at the very lowest at the duty of handing on to them an organization of society no worse than that which we ourselves inherited. But our first concern must necessarily be with the present generation.

4

Finally, any outline of an economic system which we draw up must be compatible with the democratic idea. This implies something about the nature both of the end it strives for, and of the means it employs. So far as the end is concerned, it implies that the ultimate object of all endeavour must be the greater welfare of all the people in their individual capacities. The means must be those of tolerance and discussion. A project for economic reform might increase efficiency, equity, and adaptability all at once ; but if it can be carried through only by oppression, by the denial of human rights, and by the instrumentality of brute force, then it must be forsworn. No man, and no party, can be trusted to keep the interests of the people at heart if their method is to deny the people all right to criticize their actions. This does not, of course, mean that no device can be adopted except such as will command an immediate majority vote. But it does mean that the general progress of economic reform, both in its ends and in its means, must be such as the people will freely approve. The eighteenth century tried benevolent despotism, and found that it did not work. We cannot afford to try it again.

PART TWO.—FALSE ROADS

CHAPTER IV

THE NEW FEUDALISM

THE first part of this book has sketched in the broadest outline what should be the main lines of economic progress in a democratic commonwealth. We have naturally been dealing very largely with abstractions ; the next task is to turn to an examination, which must unfortunately be equally summary, of some of the practical policies of economic progress that are being practised or advocated in Great Britain to-day.

To extend the survey to include every doctrine maintained wherever two or three people are gathered together would obviously require a work of encyclopædic dimensions. In practice there are only two alternative policies which seem at present to have any considerable likelihood of being translated into action, and these are the policies professed by the Conservative and Labour Parties. For this reason this second part of the book will be given over to an analysis of the economic programmes of these two parties. We shall start with the economic policies of the Conservative Party.

I

Historically, the Conservatives are the party of the landowners. But they have become the party of the business men. To explain how this has happened would involve an interesting chapter of social and economic history, for which we have no space. But that it is so cannot be denied. The landed gentry and the hereditary aristocrats still adorn the ranks of the Conservatives in parliament; in the House of Lords the landed interest is still supreme. But, fundamentally, the Conservative Party is a business party. That does not, of course, mean that the party has no eyes for the interests of any but a narrow class. But it does mean that the thinking of the party on economic matters is dominated by the view of those matters that can be obtained through the horn-rimmed spectacles of the company director. The business man who does not regularly cast his vote for the Conservative candidate is in these days a *rara avis*. And it needs only a perfunctory perusal of debates on economic affairs in the House of Commons to convince the most hardened doubter that the party of the landowners has been captured by the business men.

It follows quite naturally from this fact that the policy pursued by the Conservative Party is in general that which business men—that is, managers, directors, chairmen, and employers of labour—want. When the affairs of any particular industry are under review, the Conservative Party will, in the great majority of cases, follow the advice and accede to the wishes of the business men in that industry. And even in the exceptional case, where the Conservative Party, at the bidding of a Conservative Government, enacts legislation which arouses the hostility of the industry most directly concerned, the general outline of the legislation will be such as business men in other industries want. Nearly every Conservative Member of Parliament is connected more or less directly with some industry or group of industries. There are very few economic interests which do not find a spokesman in the House when their affairs are under discussion. And there are equally few Conservative members whose names do not appear in the *Directory of Directors*. The Conservative Party as a whole believes in nothing so tenaciously as in what it is pleased to call " sound business principles."

In the days when business men, left to themselves, found no difficulty in earning profits, " sound business principles " meant that the state should undertake no sort of interference with business. But times have changed. We no longer live in the rapidly and steadily expanding England of Queen Victoria. It is no longer true that every industry can do better by itself than it would with state interference. There are many industries, in fact, which depend upon state interference for their life. So the views of the business man have changed. Whatever else in the realm of economics the Conservative Party may stand for, it does not now stand for free, independent, and untrammelled private enterprise. Though business men still preach, in the abstract, the virtues of non-intervention, they mean the sort of non-intervention that Mussolini practised in Spain—intervention on their behalf to prevent their competitors from intervening. Whatever may be the traditional slogans exchanged between the two great parties to the political argument, even though the rival logicians still fight under the banners of " free private enterprise " and " socialism," the real dispute nowadays is not whether there should be intervention in the economic system by the state, but only about what sort of intervention, on whose side, and in whose interest.

The Conservative Party, then, believes in intervention for the protection of the interests of the business man and his profits. Let it be said at once that there is nothing that is necessarily unworthy in such an attitude. Every class of society sincerely believes that it deserves particular protection because it is a sort of trustee for society in the large. This is particularly so with the business man, and he can make out a strong case for his claim. So long as the state has not taken over the whole economic system in all its ramifications, the business man is the balance-wheel of the economic mechanism. If he is refused the opportunity to make profits, if he is compelled to make losses, he will be forced to reduce the scale of his activities and throw his employees out of work. If an established business, to which thousands of workers are attached, is forced through a steady run of losses to close down, there will inevitably be an immediate increase in unemployment. It can therefore always be argued that assistance given to the profits of an industry is a direct means of safeguarding the jobs of the workers, and the argument has all the more force when, as is usually the case, it is not a matter of increasing profits so much as of avoiding losses. It is easy to poke fun at this argument, to deride its moral assumptions, to question its ethical basis. The fact remains that it is true. Time and again it has been proved by experience that high profits and high employment, low profits and low employment, march hand in hand.

One of the most vitally important truths about any economic system (save the completely state-controlled) that the man in the street should realize is that adequate profits are an essential part of the mechanism. But another equally important matter is to realize the proper limitations of profits. Profits should be the reward of the imaginative investment of capital that sets the wheels of industry turning faster. He who can pay the standard rates for his labour and materials, and combine them in such a way as to produce more wealth than he has consumed, has benefited the community in earning his profits. He who misapplies capital, labour, and materials in such a way as to produce less wealth than he consumes deserves his losses as a measure of his disservice to the common good. Profits thus are, or should be, a measure of success in wealth-creating ; they are the reward to capital and enterprise for the skill required and the risk taken in managing and directing industry. It is in this sense that profits are essential to any community that we can envisage in a democratic future ; and in the next chapter we shall have to examine in more detail just how disastrous it is for any community when its profits disappear.

But this applies to profits in general, and it clearly links them with the production of wealth. The profits of an individual industry may not mean that it is efficiently co-operating in the production of wealth ; they may mean the exact opposite. The industry may be gaining its profits not by creating wealth, but by withholding it ; not by making the wheels of the economic mechanism turn faster, but by deliberately retarding them. An industry can do this in a variety of ways—by restricting its production and thus forcing the price up; or by fixing a high price below which nobody can sell, and thus restricting production. It can do so either by its own action or with the help of the state. But all these services have one common characteristic ; they involve less production of wealth than would otherwise occur.

Now this sort of profit is clearly inimical to the public interest. The farmer, by restricting the supply of food available to the community, may increase his own income. But the community of which he is a part is clearly the poorer. He has a larger slice, it is true, but of a smaller cake. Unfortunately it is to the interest of all of us as individuals to try and get a larger slice ; and no one individual is responsible for the size of the national cake. Let each industry do what it wants to, and each will try to enlarge its slice at the expense of the size of the whole cake. This is inevitably so ; it is the same correct instinct of self-preservation that leads every individual member of the audience in a theatre on fire to stampede for the exit. For if you do not stampede you will be roasted. Nevertheless, when somebody with authority insists on orderly procedure in the interests of the whole crowd, each individual's interest is served. In the economic system, orderly procedure is classically represented by the force of competition, which prevents each industry from doing what it wants and compels each to compete in wealth creation for its profits. And if, for any reason, competition fails to work, or the state removes it, the public interest demands that something be put in its place to prevent each industry in turn shrinking the cake to get a larger slice.

This long digression on the rôle of profits is designed simply to make the point that while it is right to work for the increase of profits *in general*, or at least for the maintenance of an adequate volume of profits *in general*, it is very dangerous to adopt measures to protect the profits of any industry *in particular*. For much the easiest way of increasing the profits of any individual industry (and certainly the way the industrialists themselves will choose, since it involves no effort on their part) is to encourage or allow the industry to exploit its consumers by making them pay higher prices than they would in free competition. Whether or not the restriction of production is the deliberate method of such a scheme, the inevitable result of higher prices is that less is consumed. And since the object of the whole economic machine is to increase the volume of goods and services available for consumption, restriction is a crime against the public interest.

The basic weakness of the business man's economics lies in the failure to distinguish between the rightness of profits in general and the danger of protecting particular profits. The business man, having convinced himself that an adequate volume of profits is essential in the general interest, forgets all about the general interest when he tackles one industry after another. His formula is merely to find the quickest way to increase profits in that industry. And so industry after industry is set to the merry game of restriction. What should be a badge of service to the community becomes the loot of a raid on the community. The public is asked to lend its support for its own exploitation, and the policy reaches the final paradox of expecting everybody to find greater wealth and welfare in consuming less.

Conservative economic policy can thus be said to be one of protecting particular interests against the general interest, of trying to make the parts greater than the whole. Let us have a few examples.

2

There is no more characteristic illustration of the true Conservative policy—that is, the business man's policy—

than the protective tariff which the Conservatives, after a generation of protectionist agitation, succeeded in enacting in 1932.

I do not propose here to go into the endless controversy of protection *versus* free trade. It is essentially a religious quarrel, and no arguments can, at this late date, be expected to make the slightest impression on the faith of the other side. We shall only obstruct the way to sound policy if we set out with the assumption either that no tariff can do any good or that none can do any harm. The only politically realistic question at this hour of the day is what sort of protective tariff a nation like Great Britain should give itself.

There would seem to be two ways of running a protective tariff. One is to run it deliberately in the general interest. This sort of tariff must necessarily be considered as a whole. The sort of questions that will have to be asked in connection with it are all questions of the general interest. How high can a tariff be before it starts restricting the consumption of the public by imposing higher prices, or before it induces or compels foreigners to retaliate against our exports ? Since it is in depression years that there is most risk of a flood of cheap imports ruining British industries, and at the same time least risk of prices being unduly raised by a tariff, while in boom years both conditions are reversed, is there not a case for lowering tariffs in good years ? In particular, any such system of tariff protection would make it quite clear that no industry had a prescriptive right to protection. Duties would be imposed and taken off as the interests of the whole community demanded.

The second way of running a protective tariff is to base it on the theory (which we have already examined, found fallacious, and rejected) that the best way of looking after the interests of the community as a whole is to assist each industry to higher profits at the community's expense.

Now there can be no doubt at all that the first method is the only one likely to result in a tariff that advances the interests of the community as a whole. And there can be equally little doubt that the second is the method chosen by the Conservatives.

The Import Duties Act of 1932 was, in fact, drawn up in such a way as to make any attention to the general interest peculiarly difficult. The Act provides for a 10 per cent. duty on the great majority of articles. Industries that want to have higher rates must apply to the Import Duties Advisory Committee. This provision might have been deliberately devised to prevent any consideration of the protective tariff as a whole. Parliament can push off its responsibility on to the I.D.A.C., and the Committee can content itself with an examination of one industry after another, each one treated in isolation. The Committee is, of course, supposed to bear the general interest in mind in reaching its decisions, but every circumstance conspires to make it very difficult for it to do so. The industries applying for higher rates of duty are strongly organized. They apply through well-financed trade associations, and they back up their applications with detailed technical knowledge of the industry concerned, and with impressive arrays of facts and figures. The consumer, on the other hand, is totally unorganized. Even when, as in the case of the steel industry, the consumer is not the anonymous housewife, but a number of other industries using steel in their own processes of production, the opposition is naturally weak, for these other industries are quite ready to pay more for their raw material, if they are granted the assistance of the protective tariff in passing on the additional cost to the consumer ; in short, they are usually more interested in securing protection for themselves than in opposing it for those from whom they buy their materials.

The Import Duties Act provided that applications could be made to the Import Duties Advisory Committee for reductions of tariff as well as for increases, and it is a significant commentary on the degree to which there is any organized protection of the consumer's interests that hardly a single application for decrease has ever been made to the Committee. Moreover, even if the consumer did appear to argue his case, he would have to do it without specialized knowledge, without the facts and figures, and without much possibility of employing highly-paid advocates to present his case. Besides, what form could his advocacy take ? He would have to plead that the applicant industry should not be given the degree of protection that it claimed was necessary for its continued existence. That means to say, he would have to argue that firms should be allowed to be thrown into bankruptcy, and men to be thrown out of employment; and the reasons that he could give for such a startling desire would, in the nature of the case, be of a general and abstract nature, such as that the rate of duty demanded by the applicant industry was in general too high, or that the price which, after the grant of protection, the public would have to pay for the products of the industry was, in principle, excessive ; finally, because the grant of this protection might in some indirect way cause some damage, which could not be proved, to the export trades. Thus, while the applicants for higher duties can always point to very concrete factories and precisely countable bodies of workers who will be affected by them, the opposition can only produce arguments which from the nature of the case are largely of an academic sound. The public interest, in short, will always be general, remote, and imprecise, whereas the private interest is specific, immediate, and concrete.

Even if the general argument were accepted that an excessive degree of protection would be harmful to the community, it is always next to impossible to prove the harm in an isolated case. The Committee might have been given a general instruction that any industry which required a protective duty of more than, say, 30 per cent., could be presumed to be one that the country could do without. But there is no such general instruction, with the result that the Committee is never in a position to say to any applicant industry, " The price that you ask the community to pay to safeguard your existence is too high ; the country will buy the goods you make from abroad." The industry, as things are, can justly retort, " Why pick on us ? Are we not at least of equal value to industry X or Y or Z, which you have protected ? " The Import Duties Advisory Committee, if it attempted, under the present Act, to refuse protection to applicant industries and thus to sentence them to economic death, would be in the invidious position of a judge instructed to sentence criminals without any law to guide him. It is the inevitable result of a system such as that created by the Conservative Party that every industry gets the degree of protection it needs to guarantee its existence, whether or not that existence is in the communal interest. The system has the tacit assumption that there is no degree of protection that would be excessive in the interests of the country as a whole. But it is admirably designed to serve the interests of business men. They need only prove (without an opposition to cross-examine their proof) that the tariff they ask for would benefit them, without doing direct and visible harm to any other well-organized group of business men, and they are given their tariff. Once in existence, it may be increased, but will never be diminished. It is a Business-men's Tariff, providing Protection for Profits. That is its chief aim, and that has been its chief effect.

3

The Import Duties Act was intended, of course, to cover the whole range of industries in the country. But the history of the steel industry in the last six years demonstrates that the same fundamental ideas are applied to individual industries in a Conservative " reorganiza-tion " as can be seen to perfection, in their generalized form, in the Import Duties Act.

Ever since 1918 and until very recently, steel had been a depressed industry. It had been left after the war with a productive capacity and a labour force larger than could be employed in meeting the existing demand. As a result of this long period of adversity, it had become technically inefficient. Its chief need was to re-equip itself, and there were also probably some economies to be gained by a certain degree of amalgamation of firms too small for efficient production into larger concerns. The candid observer must also confess to a strong suspicion that the governing personalities of the industry were of a low average standard of competence.

In these circumstances, the main object of any policy of intervention by the state in the concerns of the steel industry should be clear ; the state should provide whatever assistance is necessary to restore the industry to reasonable profitability while taking steps at the same time to restore it to the maximum possible efficiency. If that could be done, there should be reason to hope that the need for assistance would only be temporary. The one clearly bad policy would be to provide assistance at the community's expense, without any return in greater efficiency.

And efficiency, be it always remembered, means *economic* efficiency, not merely *technical* efficiency. For example, the industry may lay down the most modern plant, employing all the latest technical devices, and thereby increase its technical efficiency. But if the production-control and price-control of the industry are such as to keep these efficient plants working at half-speed, lest they should undercut prices, their construction will be of precisely no benefit at all to the community. The community's interest in the steel industry is to have it turn out steel as efficiently, *i.e.* with as little expenditure of capital, materials, and labour, *i.e.* as cheaply, as possible. A policy that wastes the benefits of greater *technical* efficiency in restriction of output is *economically* inefficient.

Now let us observe what the Conservative policy has been. The steel industry was one of the first to be granted a protective duty. This was of great assistance to it ; it was enabled to diminish foreign competition in the British market. Moreover, by threatening to reduce imports from foreign countries still further, the British industry was able to persuade the international steel cartel to give it a bigger export quota. Thus the state's assistance in providing the protective duty enabled the industry to expand the volume of its sales both at home and abroad.

But the state's assistance did not stop there. If the British industry had been left as a number of competing firms, the effect of the tariff might have been to increase the volume of its sales without affecting prices. But the Government decided that the chances of increasing efficiency would be greater if the industry were not competing with itself, but organized as a unit. It was therefore not merely *allowed*, but *encouraged*, to turn itself into a monopoly. Individual firms were told that they should join the appropriate Association for their own particular branch of the industry, and these Associations were joined up in the British Iron and Steel Federation. And in case any sturdy individualist was loth to comply, the Federation was given a weapon to compel compliance. It was allowed to import certain supplies of unfinished steel at a specially low rate of duty ; in other words, its members could get their raw materials cheaper than non-members.

The result of these measures has been to organize the steel industry as a tight monopoly. The price of steel is no longer determined by competition between different suppliers, but by a committee meeting in Tothill Street, Westminster. And since the committee consists of steel producers, it is the safest of safe bets that the prices thus fixed are, on the average, higher than would be the prices arrived at in free competition.

Indeed, in 1938 the prices asked for steel were so high that the consumers of steel simply stopped buying. The maintenance of steel prices at a very high level led to an astonishingly rapid decline in consumption. How it can possibly be believed that a policy which helps to reduce the industrial activity of the whole country is the right sort of policy for a state-assisted industry to follow passeth the wits of man.

Thus the steel industry has received very great benefits from the state. In return it was to reorganize itself for greater efficiency. It is very difficult to discover any traces of this reorganization. It is true that there has been a great deal of technical re-equipment. But this new plant is of no use to the community unless it results in cheaper steel being available for the consumer. And that it certainly has not done ; the prices charged for British steel in 1939 were considerably higher, relatively either to other British manufactures or to steel in other countries, than they were 10 years before. Technical efficiency, in short, has been increased without any increase in economic efficiency. Indeed, the British steel industry is being outdistanced in the race for economic efficiency both by other British industries and by foreign steel industries, and every British trade that uses steel is suffering as a result. How could there be any radical reorganization of the industry when the people who are running it are the managers of the existing firms, and when the assistance provided is sufficient to make maintenance of the *status quo* essentially comfortable ? The Government (1939) took one step, and one step only, in the attempt to procure real reorganization. The chairman of the Iron and Steel Federation was an eminent man with no connections with the steel industry, who was nominated for his post by the Government. Now, it is possible that the steel monopoly would have been run even more exclusively in the sole interest of the steel producers if there had not been an independent chairman. To that extent his presence has been a restraining influence. But the idea that the mere fact of one independent individual sitting in an office in London can make a monopoly staffed by profit-earning business men act as if the public interest were their chief concern is laughable. It can be shown to be so by a very brief examination of the behaviour of the steel monopoly.

The two chief ways in which a self-seeking monopoly can act against the public interest are, first, by keeping prices too high; and second, by resisting the entry of new men with new ideas to improve the efficiency of the industry and, by their competition, keep it up to the mark. As for prices, apart from the strong presumption that a committee of producers will fix them too high, there has been a deepening chorus of protest from all the industries that consume British steel. The most eloquent testimony has come from Lord Nuffield, himself a strong believer in and beneficiary from protectionist economics, who has declared himself tempted either to buy steel from America or to make it himself rather than submit to the prices demanded by the British monopoly.

The clearest example of the attitude taken by the steel industry to new men and new ideas was provided by the case of the Jarrow scheme. This was a scheme to build a new steel works at Jarrow to use a process—that of making basic bessemer steel—which has been inadequately exploited in this country. The best available independent testimony considered the scheme both technically and commercially sound—it was only an incidental advantage that it would provide employment for one of the most bitterly depressed towns in the country. But the new works would, of course, be in direct competition with the existing firms. The Federation, whose members are the existing firms, pronounced against it and, so tight is the monopoly, it became from that moment impossible to raise capital for a venture which would have the weight of official opposition against it. It was only after the public outcry that a truncated version of the original system was allowed to go forward. After the Jarrow scheme, the whole business of producing steel in this country is clearly marked " Private Property. Keep Out. Trespassers Will Be Prosecuted."

Thus the result of Conservative steel policy has been to confer enormous advantages on the business men of the industry. They have been granted a monopoly and assured of its exclusivity and permanence ; and they have been encouraged to use it to raise prices for their product. The policy has beyond question put large profits into the pockets of steel shareholders. And it is equally beyond question that some at least of these profits have come out of the pockets of the consumers of steel— who include, directly or indirectly, almost every inhabitant of the island. But the return that the community has received for this assistance could hardly be detected with a microscope.

It would be tempting to trace the development of the same ideas in the case of the coal industry. But we must forbear. For one thing, there is no space. And for another, the basic Act in this case was passed by the Labour Government of 1930—but only after it had been mauled by the Conservative House of Lords—so that the business of allocating responsibility to the Labour and Conservative Parties is a confusing side issue. It must suffice to say that coal, like steel, has been encouraged to form itself into a tight monopoly. It has been given the power to limit the production of its members and the virtual power to fix its own prices. It is difficult to know which to find more astonishing—the fact that the community has thus encouraged the industry supplying its most vital fuel to hold it up to ransom, or the fact that the industry needed a very great deal of encouragement before it would fully use its legal powers. However, it is now using them, with the result that consumers of coal are universally complaining of high prices. The original idea of the Act of 1930 was that these monopoly powers should be given as one part of a bargain, the other being a definite move to increase the efficiency of the industry by amalgamating mines—a remedy that almost every independent inquiry since the war has recommended. But by legal obstruction and parliamentary lobbying, the industry has consistently evaded its share of the bargain. Conservative governments have shown great strength in resisting any suggestion that there should be an inquiry into excessive coal prices. But they have yielded with alacrity whenever the industry has objected to any attempt to compel it to increase its efficiency. When the affairs of an industry are under discussion, the opinions and wishes of the company directors of that industry are, for Conservatives, the guiding lines of policy. The electorate gave the Government in 1931 a doctor's mandate to cure the country's economic ills. But when ailing industries apply at the surgery, they are allowed to write their own prescription.

There is room for one more example—perhaps the supreme example—of Conservative ideas on industrial reorganization. This is the case of milk. From almost every point of view milk is a remarkable commodity.

From the nutrition point of view its importance is that it is a very good, perhaps the best, food for human beings, especially young human beings ; and that not nearly enough of it is drunk in this country—less, in fact, than in many other countries. From the health point of view milk is a dangerous carrier of disease, especially of tuberculosis. It is essential that milk should be clean, and it is agreed that English milk is not nearly clean enough. And from the economic point of view the remarkable thing about milk is that, although most foodstuffs are cheaper in England than in most other countries, milk is dearer.

A milk policy for this country should, therefore, have three objects—to increase the consumption of milk, to make milk cleaner, and to make it cheaper. A fair return must, of course, be assured to the efficient producer and the efficient distributor of milk—but this should be a limiting factor on milk policy, not its main object. For a variety of reasons, into which there is no room to enter here (chiefly the fact that milk production is higher in summer than in winter), it is essential, or at least highly desirable, that the selling of the milk of the country should be centrally controlled. Since 1933 it has, in fact, been centrally controlled by the Milk Marketing Board. So far, so good. But here comes the supreme idiocy of Conservative policy ; for this Milk Marketing Board, with its almost dictatorial powers over the price of milk, is representative, not of all the interests concerned, not even of the state itself, but solely of the producers. Not only that, but it is elected by the producers every year, so that it cannot even serve the sole interest of the farmers with any far-sighted policies. The results have been as might have been expected. At every annual price-fixing the retail price of milk has gone up. Instead of getting cheaper, it has got dearer. The efforts to improve the cleanliness of the supply have been off-hand and miserably inadequate. And such schemes as have been adopted to increase consumption, like milk-in-schools, have had to be subsidized by the state. In 1938 the Government introduced a Milk Bill, two of whose objects were to create an independent and impartial Milk Commission (though most of the powers were to be left to the producer's Board) and to authorize local authorities to insist on the pasteurization of all milk sold in their districts. This Bill was, in truth, a very mild attempt by the community to see that, if its legal powers were to be used in organizing the sale of milk, they should not be used without some attention being paid to the community's interests. But the milk producers considered themselves outraged by any suggestion that they should have to think about anything but their own profits, and their political influence was sufficient to get the Bill withdrawn.

Truly, under Conservative rule, the British community was more planned against than planning.

4

After these few brief and inadequate examples of Conservative economic policy, we must attempt to formulate a general judgment on the policy as a whole. Is it, in general and on balance, a sound policy for a great industrial country to pursue ? Almost every economic policy has *some* elements of soundness about it ; and this Conservative policy clearly has many good points.

One of them is that it is the business-men's policy; for in any free economy much necessarily depends upon the psychology of business men. When they are feeling confident and optimistic there will be more enterprise, more employment, and more production of wealth than when they are nervous or depressed. It is therefore a point—but only one point—in the Conservative policy's favour that it tends to keep the business men happy.

Another point that, with most people, will tell in the policy's favour is that the period during which it has been applied has been a period of very rapid recovery from depression. The Conservatives came into power in the autumn of 1931; their Import Duties Act was enacted in the early summer of 1932; and the recovery began almost at the same time. But every schoolboy knows the elementary logical fallacy of *post hoc, ergo propter hoc*. Because the recovery came after the Conservative remedy was applied, it does not in the least follow that the policy and the recovery stood to each other in the relation of cause and effect. In point of fact, the British recovery of 1932–37 can be traced to three main causes—cheap food, cheap money, cheap sterling. Cheap food, because the fact that British people could get their food more cheaply in 1932 than in 1929 enabled them to spend hundreds of millions of pounds on new houses, cars, and radio sets, and touched off the boom in these and other industries making goods for consumers. Cheap money, because the low rates of interest at which money could be borrowed encouraged all sorts of construction enterprise. And cheap sterling, because the depreciation of the pound sterling helped our sorely depressed export trades and removed the incubus of currency over-valuation that had been pressing upon the country ever since the return to the gold standard in 1925. Different economists would lay different stress on each of these three; but they would, I think, be virtually unanimous that these three factors in combination produced the recovery. Now of the three, Conservative economic policy cannot lay especial claim to any. Cheap food has not been a Conservative policy, rather the reverse, since several of the agricultural expedients have raised the price of food. Cheap money dates from the conversion of War Loan by Neville Chamberlain on 1st July 1932. But any Chancellor of the Exchequer in office at that time would have adopted the same policy, and the plans had been actually laid by Mr. Chamberlain's Labour predecessor. And so far from cheap sterling being an object of the Conservative-National Government, that Government was actually formed in the vain endeavour to prevent the depreciation of the pound.

Conservative economic policy can, therefore, hardly be given the credit for the recovery of the years 1932–37. But if it did not *cause* recovery, equally it did not *prevent* it. It would be a grotesque misuse of language to condemn as disastrous a policy which coincided in time with such a rapid recovery and was in full force in the year when British industrial production and the British national income reached the highest figures they have ever attained. How, then, are we to judge the policy? This is where the abstract criteria set up in Part One of this book come in useful. We will judge Conservative economic policy by its effect on Efficiency, on Equity, and on Adaptability.

First for Efficiency. Has the Conservative economic policy resulted in a greater production of wealth for distribution among and consumption by the members of the community? Now clearly there was more wealth produced and consumed in Great Britain in 1937–38 than in 1932—more, in fact, than at any previous time. But that, as we have already seen, is not the point. Would there have been still more wealth produced if the policy of forming industries into producer-monopolies had not been followed? Let us answer that question by calling the roll of a few of the industries that have had the benefit of attention from the Conservative Government in the last few years. *Steel?* The question has only to be asked to be answered. Throughout most of 1938 the production and consumption of steel were falling off steeply because the monopoly kept prices at an unduly high level, and there has been a constant chorus of complaints from steel users of the business they have been losing because of the high cost of their raw material. *Coal?* Almost alone of European coal-producing countries, British coal output in 1937 was lower than in 1929. It is surely not a coincidence that this fact coincides with the existence of a legal restriction on output.[1] *Milk?* More milk, it is true, was produced and probably more was drunk in 1937 than in 1929. But it is only too reasonable to suppose that still more would have been drunk if the dairy farmers had not used their price control to force the retail price of milk up. *Other Agricultural Commodities?* There is restriction of output in the cases of potatoes and hops. Import quotas have limited the supply of bacon. A tax has been put on bread which, if it does not restrict the consumption of

[1] We must not forget that the quota scheme was enacted by the Labour Government in 1930. But the Act—or at least those sections of it that relate to control over output and prices—is so perfect an example of Business-man's Economics that it can legitimately be treated as a Conservative measure.

bread itself, certainly reduces the amount the housewife has left over, after buying bread, to spend on other commodities. (The fact that the bread tax is a very small one is irrelevant—so, you will remember, was the servant girl's illegitimate child.) Finally, what has been the effect of the tariff? I am ready to believe that, as a result of the tariff, more of what is consumed in this country is produced in this country. But it is surely self-evident that a tariff can only very rarely increase the quantity of goods available for consumption, and that it may very often reduce it. After all, the purpose of a tariff is to keep out cheaper foreign goods. If the British goods were equally cheap they would not need protection. And if the public is compelled to buy more expensive goods, it can only buy fewer of them. It is true that in certain cases a protected industry may be able to pay its employees higher wages, and to that extent compensate them for the higher prices of protection. (It must also be remarked in parenthesis that this is not the whole case either for or against protection; we are discussing here only its bearing on Efficiency.) But, broadly speaking, the best that can be expected of a protective tariff is that it shall not reduce the quantity of wealth available for consumption; it can hardly increase it. And if you object that the increase of the British tariff came just before one of the most remarkable periods of rapidly increasing production and consumption, I shall retort that the increase of the American tariff in 1930 came just before the most sensational collapse in production and consumption known to economic annals. Such arguments lead nowhere.

The probability is that each of the industries that has had the benefit of Conservative ministrations is contributing less to the total of wealth available for the consumption of the community than it would have done if it had not been encouraged to adopt policies of price raising and output regulation. After all, what other result could be expected? The Conservative policy, as we have seen, consists of turning one industry after the other into a private profit-earning monopoly. Now some monopolies make only moderate use of their powers; others exploit them to excessive lengths. Some monopolies try to be benevolent; others are extortionate. But no monopoly run for the benefit of its members—that is, with the principal object of increasing their profits—creates as much wealth for the community as would be produced under conditions of free competition. That proposition can be proved with an apparatus of curves and diagrams that would put Euclid to shame. But Euclid himself would call it a self-evident proposition. For if a monopoly did not restrict production—either directly by a limitation on output or indirectly by raising prices—it would have no *raison d'être* at all. Monopolies are set up only when free competition increases output (" over-production " the producers call it) or lowers prices (" cut-throat competition ") so far as to endanger profits. Now whether it is *always* wrong to reduce output is a matter we shall have to discuss in Chapter VII. At the moment we are only inquiring whether a system of private monopoly does in fact restrict the output of wealth. And the answer must clearly be that it does. By the same token Conservative policy cannot be said to be very good for Efficiency. If, during the period of Conservative ascendancy, the production of wealth—that is, the Efficiency of the economic system—has increased, that is due in the main to the great recovery in those portions of the economic system that have not been taken under the wing of the new policy.

Equity need not delay us very long. The direct object of Conservative economic policy being to protect profits, it may be assumed that profits are successfully protected. In many cases, industries pass on in higher wages the prosperity secured to them by one or other of the monopolistic devices. But it is highly unlikely that any body of employers would pass on in this way the whole of their increased profits, or even that wages would be found to increase in the same proportion as profits. The very strong presumption is that the monopoly policy does not improve but rather tends to worsen the inequality of incomes.

What contribution, finally, does Conservative economic policy make towards the regularity of the economic system—*i.e.* to the avoidance of unemployment ? In the short run between 1932 and 1937 the application of this policy may have created employment. The imposition of a protective tariff possibly created more employment in the protected industries than it destroyed in the export industries. It is probable that a country which, having previously been Free Trade in its policies, for the first time imposes a general protective tariff, does thereby increase the volume of employment available to its citizens. The other monopolistic devices almost certainly diminish the total of employment, since they all operate through a restriction of output, and a restriction of output involves a restriction of employment. But, here again, it is possible that the volume of employment provided by a monopoly, though smaller, is more regular. In the short run, therefore, it is possible, even probable, that a system of monopoly assists the regularity of the economic machine.

But the weakness of the system is precisely that it is a short-run expedient. In the long run, the regularity of the economic machine and its ability to avoid unemployment depend upon its capacity to make adjustments to changing circumstances. And so far as adaptability is concerned, it is hard to imagine anything much less adaptable than a policy which ossifies the *status quo.* How can the steel industry respond to progress if no one save the existing steel companies is allowed to build a new plant ? What sort of progress is it that builds an efficient new plant, and then keeps it operating at half-capacity so as not to embarrass the old inefficient plants ? Economic progress—the discovery of new material needs and new ways of supplying them—necessarily involves damage to established and vested interests. But if you put the control of industry in the hands of these established and vested interests, what progress can you expect ?

I have given this chapter the title of " The New Feudalism." And the sort of society which the policies pursued in the past six years would create, if they were given free rein, would be remarkably like the medieval feudal system. The root idea of that system was that the land of the country was divided up between the different feudal lords. Each baron was supreme in his own district ; he ruled it without competition ; no interlopers were permitted ; and the common people were supposed to make up in security what they lacked in freedom. In the new feudalism it is the market rather than the land that is parcelled out among the barons (they are mainly barons). Every industry is to have its rightful ruler, who is to rule without competitors and do what he thinks fit, subject only to shadowy control from the state—the more shadowy because the barons, as often as not, dominate the king. The baron is supposed to be responsible for the welfare of his villeins, the consumers ; but it is only reasonable to suppose that he looks after his own interests first. Some of the new baronial rulers even have their private courts, in which they can impose fines on their subjects for failing to obey their edicts. The system has all the advantages of feudalism : everybody knows his place, and has security of tenure. But it also has the disadvantages of feudalism, the chief of which is that power is placed in the hands of those who are satisfied with the state of things as they are. Feudalism and Progress have never marched together.

CHAPTER V

LABOUR ECONOMICS: OR THE CAKE
AND THE SLICE

I

IN this chapter we must turn from the economic policy pursued during recent years of office by the Conservative Party to the chief alternative—the policy to be pursued by the Labour Party on their obtaining a majority in parliament.

The first necessity is to make it clear that we are talking in this chapter about the policies of the Labour Party, and not about Socialism. The great economic debate in this country for decades past, as has already been mentioned, has been the quarrel between two things known as " free private enterprise " and " socialism." The terms are to a very large extent unreal abstractions. We have seen in the last chapter how little the Conservatives to-day believe in that " free private enterprise," which they still continue to preach. Similarly, the Labour Party, though it professes Socialism, practises something which might in easily imaginable circumstances be something very different. Socialism and Labourism are not necessarily contradictory expressions (as Conservative policy and " free private enterprise " are), but they might easily become quite clearly divergent.

87

A Socialist economic system, on the widest definition of the word, would be a system under which industry was not run for private profit, but for the social gain of the whole community. But, on the narrow definition that is usually attached to the word nowadays, Socialism has become identified with the ownership of capital either directly by the state or by public bodies on behalf of the state. Moreover, the word connotes not merely the public ownership of capital, but public management of industry as well. In the more refined versions of Socialist policy the management of industry is to be carried out by autonomous bodies, free from day to day supervision by the Government, but there is always provision for ultimate control by the state, and the more recent versions of Socialism do not affect the main point that in a Socialist community industry would be both owned and managed by the community.

You will hear Socialism, as it is broadly defined, preached from every Labour platform in the country. But, in spite of that, the actual policy of a Labour Government equipped with a parliamentary majority would be likely to be something rather different. The Labour Party is entirely dominated by the trade unions. They provide its finances, and at its annual conferences they control a block of votes which overwhelms any non-trade union elements in the party. On any issue on which they choose to assert themselves the trade unions have absolute mastery of the Labour Party. In the same way the majority of Labour Members of Parliament are connected more or less directly with the unions. If the Conservative Party is a party of business men, and if its policy is that favoured by business men, then it follows much more strongly that the Labour Party is a party of trade unions, and that its policy is likely to be a trade union policy. No realist in the Labour ranks can deny this conclusion.

To a very large extent a Socialist policy serves the ends of the trade unions. And this is particularly true so long as the Labour Party is the opposition in a predominantly Capitalist economy. In such circumstances both the trade unions and the Socialists are working for very much the same ends. The elimination of the private owner of capital and of the profits on which he feeds can be represented as bringing both the Socialist commonwealth (in which the Socialists are interested) and higher wages (in which the trade unions are interested) appreciably closer. Furthermore, schemes for the public control of industry can very easily be amended to provide for that substantial element of trade union participation in control which is one of the fundamental objects of the trade union movement. Thus there is no reason why in the preliminary stages Socialism and trade unionism should not march in step. But that their ultimate objectives can be very different can be easily seen from Soviet Russia. Russia, so we are told, in spite of all its imperfections and doctrinal compromises, is the closest approximation to a Socialist experiment that the world has ever seen. Though he may dislike the political terrorism by which Russia is ruled, the Socialist recognizes in Russian economic policy a genuine attempt to put his own ideals into practice. It is at least true that in Russia all capital is owned by the state, that the individual capitalist has been liquidated, and that the system is run deliberately, and even self-consciously, in the interests of the worker.

But if Soviet Russia thus has a strong family resem-

blance to the Socialist ideal, it has no resemblance at all
to the trade union ideal. There are, indeed, in Soviet
Russia bodies bearing the title of trade unions. But
they are entirely subservient to the party state, and there
is nothing that a British trade unionist would recognize
as genuine collective bargaining. How could there be
a bargain when only one opinion is permitted ? So far
as the trade unions are concerned, the fiat of the employer is more absolute in Russia than in any capitalist
country. Moreover, the Soviet State infringes another
trade union principle. It is the obvious objective of
trade union action to secure that the worker should
receive in wages for his immediate consumption, or at
least for his own free disposal, the highest possible
proportion of the total value of goods and services
created by the economic machine in which he works.
But the rulers of Soviet Russia have decreed that their
state shall accumulate capital more rapidly than has ever
been done before by a community of comparable size
and poverty. Figures to decide the matter are non-
existent, but it is at least probable that the Soviet worker
receives for his immediate consumption a smaller proportion of the total value he creates than he did before the
Bolshevist revolution. The balance goes to the creation
of capital, which will, it is hoped, in the future increase
the income of all the workers. The Russian worker
may have no tribute to pay to the capitalist ; but he pays
a tribute to capital so heavy that it has frequently, in the
past twenty years, brought him close to starvation. This
may be a policy soundly conceived in the interests of the
Russian citizen, but it is none the less a policy such as
any free trade union would whole-heartedly oppose.
Thus Soviet Russia, though it acts as a magnet for all

LABOUR ECONOMICS

Socialist thinkers, has never received hearty trade union approval. Indeed, those leading British trade unionists who have visited the country have been outstanding in their criticism of the value of the Soviet experiment.

We shall not, therefore, in this chapter make the mistake of assuming that Socialism is the beginning and the end of Labour policy. It may be so for the handful of Socialist intellectuals, but for the bulk of the Labour Party, and especially for its trade union rank and file, Socialism is merely a means to an end. The end itself is higher wages, shorter hours, the closed shop, and a very much greater share of the control of industry for the representatives of the workers. These are the real aims of Labour policy.

There is thus the sharpest cleavage of economic interest between the two major parties of the state. The Conservatives are predominantly the party of business men, and the element of the national income which attracts their chief attention is profits. The Labour Party, on the other hand, is dominated by the trade unions, and its first thoughts go to wages. The dominant element in each party, it may be noted, is a minority. The number of business men in the sense in which we have been using the word—that is, directors, managers, financiers, and others actively engaged in the management of business —cannot be more than a few score thousands. Even if we add in those people who, though they do not engage in the active management of industry, are, nevertheless, mainly dependent upon dividends, we shall still hardly have reached a million people. The eight million or more people who vote Conservative are certainly not all business men, in this or any other sense. Nevertheless they follow the lead, within the party, of business men, and their representatives in Parliament include a larger proportion of business men than their members throughout the country. Similarly, in the Labour Party, the trade unions behind the party (1939) have a membership of only 4,460,000, which is far less than the eight million Labour voters, and even more strikingly out of proportion to the twenty million wage-earners of the country. There is a strong general presumption that the policy pursued by the minority of business men accords fairly well with the economic interests of the Conservative voters, and similarly that the policy pursued by the trade union minority accords fairly well with the interests of the Labour voters. But it is no more than a general presumption. The hard realism of the matter is that with the present constitution of our existing major parties the country is ruled alternately by each of two small minorities, the minority of company directors and the minority of trade union officials. (Any such statement of the case would, however, be misleading if it failed to recognize the fact that a still larger and more continuous influence is exerted by an even smaller minority, the Civil Service.)

What is discussed in the remaining sections of this chapter, then, is the Labour policy of higher wages, shorter hours, and extended trade union control of industry, and not the Socialist formula of nationalization. Nationalization of industry is excluded here for three reasons. In the first place, it will have to be fully discussed in later chapters ; secondly, even the most fervent Socialist recognizes that complete nationalization of all industry will take several decades, if not generations, and the Labour movement must have some economic policy for the intervening period. And thirdly, even after complete nationalization there will still remain a labour problem for the trade unions, and the Labour Party they control will still have to represent the interests of the workers, even though their opposite numbers will then be the salaried managers of nationalized industries rather than the profit-earning directors of private companies.

When Labour policy is approached from this angle we have very little actual experience to go upon, for the two first Labour Governments which have existed in this country had no majority in Parliament to carry out their policy, and tended to act rather like timid Liberal Governments. But if we go beyond the shores of Great Britain there have been two recent examples of Governments attempting to pursue the Labour programme. These were, of course, the experiments of F. D. Roosevelt in the United States and M. Blum in France. Neither government (least of all Roosevelt's) acted exactly as a British Labour Government would act. But both of them have deliberately used both legislation and also the strong administrative pressure of the Government to secure the trio of trade union demands—higher wages, shorter hours, and a trade union voice in the control of industry. They can therefore be regarded as Labour Governments, even though Roosevelt would have been horrified at the title of Socialist. The results of their experiments will serve as a useful check on the conclusions at which we arrive in our analysis of Labour policies.

2

Let us take up the last of the three objectives, the desire of the trade unions to have an increased say in the control of industry. In the main, the control they desire is of a negative rather than a positive character. It is true that some of the earlier Labour plans for the nationalization of industry provided for strong trade union representation, or even a majority, on the board or committee which was to run the nationalized industry. But these somewhat exaggerated demands have now been largely abandoned, and the desire of the unions is now only to control absolutely the wages earned and hours worked by the workers in their industries, and in particular to exercise an equal degree of control over the conditions of recruitment and employment.

These desires are wholly natural and legitimate, and no trade union can be blamed for seeking such control, or exercising it when it is able. Nevertheless, this aspect of trade union policy has two dangers, both of which tend to reduce the efficiency of the economic mechanism.

The first danger is that a trade union movement tends to be as particularist as the modern Conservative Party, if not more so. We have seen in the last chapter that the views of the Conservative Party on the reorganization of an industry tend in almost every case to be the views of the business men in that industry. Similarly, the views of the trade union movement on the reorganization of an industry tend to be the views of the trade union in that industry. When any question of coal comes up, the Labour Party follows the lead of the Mine Workers' Federation, while in matters concerning the railways it leaves the formulation of Labour policy very largely in the hands of the three Railway Unions.

It follows from this tendency that the process of turning one industry after another into a self-governing monopoly, which we have seen at work in the last chapter, is not likely to be strongly opposed by the trade union movement. On the contrary, they support it, and their only quarrel with the Tory brand of monopoly is a quarrel about who shall reap its benefits.

This tendency was very closely revealed during the important debates on the Coal Bill in the early months of 1938. One of the hottest subjects of controversy during these debates was whether or not the cartelized coal industry could be fairly accused of extorting excessive prices from the consumers of coal. The controversy centred round a proposal that a public inquiry should be held into the working of the coal-selling schemes, to determine whether or not they were being used by the industry to force the price of coal up to an unreasonable level. This was the clearest possible example of an antagonism between the interests of the community as a whole and those of a particular industry. And it was highly significant that the Labour Party, following the lead of its mining members, voted for the industry and against the public. This incident is not perhaps entirely typical, since the miners have an unusually powerful influence on Labour policy, and also because there is a profit-sharing arrangement in the mining industry by which the workers share immediately in any greater prosperity of the employers. But the incident is sufficient to show that the trade unions cannot be relied upon to prevent the tendency towards the creation of neo-feudal monopolies, the dangers of which were pointed out in the last chapter.

Trade union aspirations for control usually work more directly in the industrial field than through their political activities. In almost every industry the trade unions have set up rules which tend in the interests of their members to increase the costs of production, and thus to diminish the output of the industry concerned. In some industries the aim of these rules is to spread the available work over the largest possible number of men— as in the newspaper printing industry, where the unions insist on more than twice as many men being employed at a printing press as are required efficiently to run it. In other industries the rules attempt to limit the number of men in the industry by means of restrictions on apprenticeship and the like. Examples of this sort of rule can also be found in the printing trades and in all forms of engineering and construction work. The object is, of course, to give the labour of the favoured few admitted to the industry a scarcity value.

Let it be repeated that there is nothing reprehensible or morally wrong in these practices. They are indeed very natural measures adopted to serve the self-interest of the members of the unions, and they are certainly no worse than the great variety of monopolistic and restrictive practices adopted by employers or by the professions. But that does not alter the fact that they are not such as the community ought to encourage, or such as ought to form part of a consistent policy for enriching the commonwealth. Least of all they should be associated with any body of precepts which appears under the name of Socialism, for they are all attempts by tiny minorities or vested interests to exploit the advantages of the situation in which they are placed to extort from the community a larger living for themselves in return for no greater contribution to the common pool of goods and services by which the community lives. Their effect, in a word, is anti-social rather than social. They are phenomena of un-Socialism rather than of Socialism.

3

The next aim of Labour policy which we shall pass under review is the reduction of working hours. There are two questions which must be asked : Is it in the interest of the wage-earners that their hours of work should be reduced ? and secondly, Is it in the interest of the community as a whole that the standard hours of work should be shortened ?

Let us first clear out of the way a few confusing side issues. There are a number of industries in which the workers would actually be able to produce more if they worked for shorter hours. Two decades ago, when throughout industry the hours of work were reduced from an average of about 60 to an average of about 48, it was discovered in several industries that the average man or woman could in fact do just as much work, if not more, in 48 hours a week as he or she had previously accomplished in 60 hours a week. It may very well be that there are some industries in which the same result would follow on a further reduction of hours—particularly so if the reduction took the form, not of the shortening of the average day, but of the elimination of Saturday morning work or the extension of paid holidays. If so, this reduction of hours ought unquestionably to be undertaken, since it would give added leisure to the workers without operating against the interests of anybody else. But at the same time it must be recognized that the number of cases in which this is true must be comparatively few. After all, it cannot be true that production will increase with every reduction of hours. There cannot be any industries in which more would be produced in a two-hour day than in an eight-hour day. And the shorter the hours that are worked already, the less likely it is that any further reduction would lead to an increase of output. Moreover, it is only likely to be true in industries engaged in manufacture, which are now a minority of the total. In summary, we may say that every industry ought to experiment with its hours, especially with paid holidays, to see whether in fact they can be reduced without any damage being done to output.

Secondly, there are a number of industries which are still working excessively long hours—longer, that is to say, than the average of other industries. Some of these cases are quite scandalous. For example, the hours worked by page boys and messenger boys in our cities have been discovered by an official inquiry to exceed in some cases 66 hours a week. This sort of thing ought immediately to stop. Every industry's hours ought, on the grounds of fairness alone, to be brought down to the national average, which is now about 45 hours a week ; and in industries where the work is peculiarly arduous or damaging to health hours should, for that reason, be shorter than the national average.

All these, however, are exceptions to the general rule. After we have reduced hours throughout industry to 45 a week, and after each industry has experimented to see whether the five-day week and holidays with pay can be instituted without reducing output—only then can we approach the real problem of shorter hours. Should the standard week be reduced from 48 hours to 40 hours in that great majority of industries where such a reduction would mean a diminution in the average worker's weekly output? That is the real problem of shorter hours.

If the average worker after a reduction of hours is producing less in a week than he used to, and if also he is not to consume less, it follows with quite mathematical exactitude that his consumption must be subsidized from some other source. The whole community cannot produce less and yet consume as much as before. If, therefore, some succeed in reducing their production without reducing their consumption, it follows that other members of the community must be doing the opposite, *i.e.* consuming less whilst producing as much as before. Let us translate the argument from abstract terms into concrete ones. Let us suppose that throughout industry hours are reduced from 48 a week to 40, *i.e.* by one-sixth. Now if the weekly pay-envelope of the average worker is reduced in the same proportion, his purchasing power and his standard of living are automatically cut down by one-sixth. But when the trade unions advocate shorter hours they do not in the least mean this. They mean that the worker must receive the same pay-envelope for working 40 hours as he formerly received for working 48 hours. If he receives the same money for doing less work, it follows that the cost of production to his employer has gone up. In the normal course of events prices will similarly rise, and the worker runs the risk of finding that although he still receives the same number of shillings a week in his pay-envelope, they will purchase less than before. Thus, if his wages are reduced, his purchasing power suffers directly and immediately, and even if his wages are not reduced it is highly likely that his purchasing power will suffer indirectly ; in either case, shorter hours mean less to eat. This result can only be avoided if by some means prices can be prevented from rising. That involves the assumption that employers are to meet the increase in their costs of production without themselves increasing the prices they charge. In other words, the workers can have their hours of work reduced, and not themselves suffer any reduction of consumption, only if employers can be persuaded or compelled to meet the extra costs of production out of their own profits. We will shortly return to this matter of profits, to investigate whether they can in fact be squeezed in this way.

There is, however, another argument in favour of shorter hours which is very frequently heard in periods of depression. This is that the hours worked by the man or woman in employment should be reduced in order to provide work for the unemployed. Thus, if there are 100 men in a factory working 48 hours a week, there can be said to be 4,800 man-hours of work available. And if no worker is allowed to work for more than 30 hours, there will be work for 160 men. This, at least, is the argument, and we may ignore the manifold practical complications which immediately suggest themselves in order to analyse the principle underlying it. Fundamentally this principle is one of spreading work over a larger total of workers. From the point of view of the man who has his hours of work reduced from 48 to 30, it does not differ in the least from the case we have just been discussing. Either his wages are reduced, or if they are not, there is a strong presumption that the prices of the things he buys will rise. The unemployed, of course, gain, since they are given work and wages which, though they may be low in purchasing power, are possibly greater than the dole. But the net effect of the whole procedure is to transfer the burden of maintaining the unemployed from the state, which was previously paying them the dole, to the workers, who have suffered a reduction in their own purchasing power in order to provide work for the unemployed. When this proposal is analysed, it differs very little from a proposal to put the burden of unemployment on the shoulders of the wage-earner instead of on those of the income-tax payers. It is not one that the representatives of labour ought to countenance.

The proposal of shorter hours is therefore a much more dubious one than appears at first sight. So far as the community is concerned, it implies that the individuals who compose the community are deliberately choosing to have more leisure at the cost of less income. Now, this is a perfectly legitimate choice ; and if the community really believes that it is relatively so well supplied with the material good things of life that it prefers to call a halt in their increase, and take the next instalment of progress in the shape of longer hours of leisure, nobody will wish to criticize the decision. The advent of leisure in the last few decades has made an enormous and, on balance, a beneficial difference to life for the great mass of the people. Moreover, many of the great inventions and developments of the modern age, such as the cinema, radio, motor transport, and the like, are such as require increased leisure for their full enjoyment. Thus, if the

community deliberately chooses leisure rather than
income, there is much to applaud in the decision.

But does it so choose ? Has the choice ever been
clearly put to the individuals who compose the modern
community ? Has it ever been made clear to them that
it is in fact a choice between leisure and income ? The
answer to all three questions is surely, No. The wage-
earners have been led to believe that there is some
magical means by which they can secure more leisure at
once without sacrificing any of their present income—
some mysterious economic alchemy by which, although
each one of the citizens of a community produces less,
the community as a whole nevertheless has no less to
consume. If this delusion were once cleared out of the
way, it is very doubtful indeed whether there would be
much pressure for a reduction in the standard hours of
work. If the average working man were told that he
could look forward over the next few years *either* to an
increase in his standard of living *or* to a reduction in his
hours of work, but not to both, and if he were asked
which he would prefer to have, it is so probable as to be
almost certain that he would choose the increased
standard of living. From the point of view of the community that conclusion is almost imposed by the facts of
the case. As a community we are still so poor that the
most rapid possible increase in our material income must
rank as one of the first objectives of economic policy. It
could be waived in favour of shorter hours of work only
if it could be shown that the standard hours of work
were so excessively long as to prevent the workers from
enjoying their material incomes. But that is manifestly
not the case. There are 168 hours in the week, and it is
not unreasonable to expect the average man to work

48 hours out of the total, so long as one of the chief needs of the community is to increase wealth. For the individual worker in the individual industry this argument will only cease to apply if there is some possibility of his trade union leaders being able to force the employers to give up some of their profits for his benefit. And even if those circumstances did exist, they would work just as strongly in favour of an increase of wages, which the average worker would greatly prefer.

Why, then, if a reduction of hours would mean a reduction in the standard of living, do so many people devotedly advocate it? The first and most obvious reason is that they have never thought the matter out clearly. They have been deluded by catchwords such as that "the problem of production is solved" into believing that it is possible for the community to produce less and yet consume more. It must be said that many propagandists of the Labour Party who ought to know better have assisted in building up this colossal delusion that the income of the community can somehow be plucked out of the air, or derived from some source other than the community's own work.

And secondly, it is true that in some individual industries it may be possible for the workers to secure a reduction of hours without any reduction of wages simply because the industry as a whole can charge more for its products. But this is true only when the industry is in a monopoly position—when, that is to say, it is in a position to extort more from the community for its goods, and the increased leisure of its workers is provided entirely out of the pockets of the rest of the community. That an individual industry in such a position should take full advantage of its position is very natural. But its success in so doing is neither an argument that other industries can do likewise nor a proof that such action is in the common interest.

4

The raising of wages is obviously a different matter from the shortening of hours. For one thing, there is clearly a limit to the reduction of hours, save perhaps in the totally mythical Utopia in which everything can be done by pressing a button, without there being any need even for labour to man the machines. But for wages the sky is the limit. And, for another thing, the reduction of hours is at least potentially a restriction of production, which is the source of wealth, while wages are the reward for increasing productivity.

The argument for higher wages is thus on far surer ground than the argument for shorter hours. In fact, there is an invincible case for a gradual rise in wages. The productivity of the average man, aided by the ingenuities of the scientist and the engineer, has been increasing for some two centuries now, and is still increasing, at an average rate of about 1 per cent. per annum. Booms and slumps come and go, and periods of rapid advance give way to intervals of stagnation. But the average reasserts itself with astonishing consistency. This being so, the *minimum* advance in the wages and in the real standard of living of the average working man should work out at the same average of 1 per cent. per annum. That is the rock-bottom case for higher wages.

But is that all? Is there a case for a faster rate of increase? Are the trade unions right in forcing a more rapid advance ? In particular, is it right to advocate an increase in wages as a cure for depression ? This is the Labour doctrine that has been put into practice both in America and France in recent years. The argument in favour of it is attractive. It runs like this : " What is a depression ? A state of affairs in which the community does not buy all the goods it could produce. And why does it not buy as much as it might ? Because the members of the community do not possess enough income or purchasing power to offer a fair price for all the goods. Therefore, to cure the paradox of poverty in the midst of plenty, let us make sure that the majority of the individual members of the community, *i.e.* the wage-earners, get increased purchasing power. Let us increase wages and all will be well."

That is the argument. Let us examine it. But let us first make an absolutely crucial distinction—the distinction between wages and wage-rates. Wage-rates are what are increased—a wage-rate is what has to be paid to a worker in return for an hour's, a day's, or a week's work. But the individual worker's income consists, not of wage-rates, but of wages ; and his earnings depend partly upon the rate per hour and partly on the number of hours' work he gets. Similarly, the total income of the working class depends partly upon the level of wage-rates and partly upon the amount of unemployment. When the Labour theorists say that an increase of the purchasing power of the wage-earners would cure depression, they mean an increase in wages, *i.e.* in the total income of the working class, what the Americans call pay-rolls. But when they say " Raise wages," they mean " Raise wage-rates."

Are the two things the same ? The whole Labour case

assumes that they are, and that an increase in wage-rates will automatically raise wages. But this is a very doubtful assumption. The wage-rate is the price of a given amount of labour, and an increase in the price of most commodities at the bottom of depression would lead not to an increase but to a fall in the amount of money spent on them. Indeed, any business man will tell you that the soundest policy (*i.e.* the one that attracts the greatest demand) in depression time is to reduce prices as far as possible. Now to many people it is distasteful to speak of labour as a commodity. But it is unlikely that verbal squeamishness will alter the fact that the amount of labour that people will buy is influenced by the price charged for it. This being so, an increase in wage-rates may lead either to an increase in wages or to a fall.

Now if it leads to an actual decrease in wages, the whole argument clearly falls to the ground, since the working class will then have less purchasing power, not more, and depression will be deepened. Do not be so foolish as to dismiss this as a purely theoretical argument. It is easy to show that a general increase in wage-rates in the United States in 1933 did, in fact, lead to a fall in wages. But there are other cases in which the opposite seems to have happened. Let us follow out what happens then. Let us assume that wage-rates have been raised, and that, as a result, the working class as a whole has a larger money income to spend on consumption. Clearly the increase in wage-rates means an increase in costs of production, and the natural reaction would be a rise in prices. If the rise in prices is as large as the rise in wage-rates, then the real benefit to the individual worker will be nil, since his larger income will be swallowed up in higher costs of living. And if the rise in prices is not as large as the rise in wage-rates, the employer's profits must be suffering, for the worker, without producing any more, is consuming more. It follows that somebody must be consuming less; and that somebody is inevitably the great residuary legatee—the profit-earner.

So wage-raising (apart from the gradual rise that comes from greater productivity) comes back to the same point as hour-shortening—the worker benefits only if it is possible to restrict profits. These Labour policies are in the interest of the wage-earner only if they are against the interest of the profit-receiver. This is, of course, not in the least conclusive. Generally speaking, the wage-earner is a more deserving creature than the profit-receiver, and it may be a good idea to hand over part of the latter's slice of the cake to the former. But that leads us at last to the investigation into the importance of profits which has been so often promised in this chapter and the last.

Let us give it a new section.

5

There are many definitions of the word " profits," all of them useful for particular purposes. For our own particular purpose profits are what goes into the pockets of the managers of industry after they have paid wages and salaries to their employees, rent to their landlords, and interest to their creditors. It is essentially a composite item. There is frequently an element of wages in it, as the profit-receivers often put in plenty of hard work at their job of management. There is an element of interest, since the profit-earners have usually invested capital in the business. There is often an element of rent in profits, since many firms' profits come from the exploitation of a pseudo-monopoly position from which, like the landlord who owns a coveted piece of land, they can levy toll on the public. But perhaps the largest element in profits is that of pot luck, for the essential characteristic of profits is that they are the residuary element that is left when others have had their share.

It so happens that the greater part of profits goes to rich men. Not all, by any manner of means. There is the host of small business men, down to the owner of the smallest fish-and-chip shop, who live on profits, but are in no way rich. Then there are the thousands of poor or moderately poor who own a few shares in one or more public companies ; their income also comes partly or wholly from profits. But when we talk of profit-receivers, we mean in the main the race of business men who supply the fibre of the Conservative Party, men whose income is distinctly above the average. Now this is a most unfortunate confusion. It is almost impossible to separate in one's mind the two logically quite distinct notions of " incomes from profits " and " large incomes." But the effort to draw the distinction must be made if clear thought on the question is not to be quite impossible. You may hate the rich, and be longing for their extermination ; but still it does not follow that because the rich live on profits, profits themselves are detestable. After all, many of the least likeable parasites in the world of vermin live on human blood ; but nobody would argue from that fact that blood itself should be drained out of the human body.

Let us, therefore, for the moment try to forget about the rich and concentrate on profits. Let us, if you like, agree for the sake of argument that the rich are quite unnecessary. And let us inquire what is the necessity for profits. Whenever economists have nothing else to argue about, they sit down to argue whether it is possible to imagine a completely state-owned economic system in which there would be no profits. I think it is fully possible to imagine such a system (though perhaps less possible actually to devise an economic system in which positive profits or negative profits—*i.e.* losses—would not bob up). But there is not the slightest need for us to stop at the moment to explore this fascinating by-way of theoretical economics. This book is concerned with what can be done by the present generation in a democratic state ; and if one thing is certain it is that a very large part of the national economy in a democracy is going to continue to be managed by private firms for at least the lifetime of our generation—if only because the effort of nationalizing everything in a hurry would smash the democratic system. And even within that gradually extending sector of the national economic system where industry is socialized, the centralized control, the nationalized corporation, the public board— call it what you will—is expected to make profits. This may seem a hard saying ; but it is not so when it is remembered that making profits is only the same thing as avoiding losses. Even the most brilliant accountant cannot make a public board's income exactly equal its outgo ; and if the difference is not to be a loss, it must be a profit.

For an economy of this sort—partly privately owned, partly in the hands of public bodies instructed at least to avoid losses—profits are essential, whatever they might be in a Socialist Utopia. Just *why* they are essential, however, is very frequently misunderstood. It is frequently argued as if the average capitalist, finding his rate of profit too low, will deliberately cut down the scale of his operations, sack some of his employees, and generally draw in his horns, perhaps even go out of business entirely if his profits continue to be inadequate. Just as a worker will not work if the wage is too small— so one might imagine to listen to these accounts of how things work—a capitalist will not do his job if his profits are too small. Actually this is a very false picture. Most business men will go on doing their jobs so long as there is any profit at all. Even if there are actual losses, the business usually continues. It usually pays a business man to suffer losses for one, two, three, or more years rather than abandon his capital completely. And even when he is forced into bankruptcy, somebody else buys up his business at a bankrupt price and continues to run it. If anybody believed that inadequate profits would lead business men to be less willing to stay in business, they should look at the history of the Lancashire cotton industry since the war.

What, then, is the necessity for profits ? It is not that business men refuse to play when their profits are inadequate. The reason is more profound than that. If the profits that are being made in any industry or in any individual firm are inadequate it will be impossible to raise fresh capital for that industry or firm. Let us suppose that £100,000 has been invested in a flour mill. When it was invested it was presumably expected to earn a profit of at least £5,000 a year. Now, if the actual profit turns out to be only £1,000, it will be more profitable to keep the mill running than to close it down. Even if the profit is a loss of £1,000 a year, the owner will probably prefer to suffer it rather than abandon his mill, which would, in effect, be a loss of £100,000 instead of £1,000. But, so long as the profits are less than about £5,000, nobody in his senses would invest any money in an extension of the mill or in the construction of a similar mill. And if the community is at that stage of the trade cycle where profits in *all* industries are low, then there will be little or no investment of capital in industry.

But if the investment of capital comes to a stop, the savings of the community are running to waste. The community, let it be remembered, cannot accumulate wealth in the form of money. So far as the community is concerned, unless saving is immediately incorporated in some tangible form of durable wealth it is wasted. And when savings are not being converted into capital, that is the same thing as saying that part of the public's income is not being spent. The demand for goods is less than the supply of them, and general depression is the result.

The argument can be translated into less abstract language. Industries can be divided into two categories according as the things they produce are wanted for immediate consumption (consumers' goods) or are wanted by producers to help them make consumers' goods. Flour-milling is a consumers' industry, since flour is wanted for immediate consumption. But the manufacture of milling machinery is a producers' industry, as nobody "consumes" milling machinery. Now the existing flour mills will be kept at work so long as people are eating bread, whether the owners of the flour mills are making a profit or not. But the manufacturers of milling machinery will be kept busy only so long as people are building *new* flour mills or buying new machinery for the old mills. Accordingly, if there is no profit in flour milling, there will be no employment in the milling machinery industry. And the unemployed machine-makers will eat less bread, so that there will be still less profit in flour-milling. So the vicious spiral of depression works itself out.

The basic reason for an adequate volume of profits is, then, that without it there will not be an adequate volume of new capital investment, and without an adequate volume of new capital investment there will be unemployment and slump. Now please note three things about this argument. *First*, it applies not only to what is usually called " the Capitalist system," but also to any Socialist system which attempts to allocate its supplies of capital among the different industries according to the useful employment they can make of it. In other words, it applies to almost any conceivable Socialist system—certainly to every Social-Democratic system. *Second*, it is a completely non-ethical and amoral argument. It does not say that profits *ought* to exist, or that the profit-receiver does anything for which he *ought* to receive a reward. It merely points out that if profits are inadequate, certain things are likely to happen, among them widespread unemployment. *Third*, it does not in the least maintain that profits can never be reduced without a slump resulting. In individual industries profits can be and frequently are excessive—by " excessive " meaning so high that they can be reduced without loss, and possibly with advantage to the community. Indeed, the whole argument of the previous chapter of this book was directed to showing that the normal result of the policy pursued by the Conservative Party in recent years was to protect certain individual excessive profits. It is also fully possible for there to be times when not merely the profits of individual industries, but the profits of nearly all industries, are excessive. That was almost certainly true of the United States in the years 1927–29. If profits are reduced at such a time, either by all-round wage increases or by other means, no harm to the community will result. But there are other times when general profits are too low, and when, in consequence, the construction industries are bitterly depressed. To reduce profits at such a time is to deepen depression and increase unemployment.

This is where we come back to the Labour policies of shortening hours and/or raising wages. We have seen in the two previous sections of this chapter that these policies can succeed in increasing the welfare of the workers only if they succeed in reducing the margin of profits. Since neither shorter hours nor higher wages do anything to increase the size of the cake produced by the industrial system, a larger slice can only be got for the workers by imposing a smaller slice on the profit-receivers. It clearly emerges from our discussion that these policies are sometimes right and sometimes wrong. When profits are high and business is booming, the Labour movement is not merely within its rights in demanding higher wages, it is conferring a positive benefit on the community by doing so. The justification for such action is not the ethical one that the profit-receivers are getting more than their " fair " share, but the strictly practical one that the wage-earners can then get more without hurting the community (*i.e.* themselves) by starting a depression. And by reversing all these arguments it can be shown that to ask for higher wages or shorter hours when profits are below the balancing-

point is not wrong so much as stupid, since it creates
unemployment. It is doubly stupid for a Labour Party
in office, since mounting unemployment will push it out
of power.

The great defect of Labour policy is that it does not
distinguish between right times and wrong times.
Indeed, higher wages and, more particularly, shorter
hours are preached more vehemently at the wrong times
(*i.e.* at the bottom of depressions) than at the right
times.

This mistaken attitude of mind arises directly from the
failure of Labour politicians to appreciate the rôle of
profits. Confusing, as they do, profit incomes with large
incomes, the Labour politicians have made an enemy
out of profits. Profits, they argue (or it would be more
accurate to say they assume without argument), are an
evil—perhaps a necessary evil so long as the capitalist
system cannot be reformed out of existence, but still an
evil. This is a profound mistake. The policy that would
bring most benefit to the wage-earners would be one
that set itself to see that profits, on the average of all
industries, were always up to the point at which a steady
stream of new capital investment would be undertaken.
On the political side, by reducing unemployment, this
policy would secure the continuance in office of the party
that pursued it. On the economic side, by ensuring that
rapid expansion of productivity which the steady investment of new capital creates, it would open the way for
an equally rapid increase in the standard of living of the
workers.

Let me repeat that the maintenance of profits is an
entirely different matter from the maintenance of large
incomes. It is fully possible to maintain profits, and yet

to impose such heavy taxation on the rich that all large incomes are severely reduced. It would be wrong to say that heavy taxation on large incomes has *no* effect on the activity of industry. Almost certainly it has *some* effect ; but quite certainly it has much less effect than a policy of stamping out profits. To allow profits to arise and then tax high incomes is a policy of levelling incomes *up*, since it gives industry a chance to provide high employment, and high wages, for the workers. But the attempt to get rid of profits at the source is a policy of levelling incomes *down*, since it is likely to do as much harm to the workers as to the rich.

The argument of this chapter has been very simplified in order to bring the main points out. A number of minor qualifications, modifications, and exceptions have been ignored in order not to clutter the main thread. For example, we have argued as if the workers and the profit-receivers were the only people who received a slice of the industrial cake, and we have ignored the possibility of reducing the slices going to such people as creditors and landlords. Such a possibility does exist ; if prices rise, these gentry will have a lower income *in goods*, although they still receive the same income *in money* that they contracted for. But this chapter is already so very long that you will have to take my word for it that while this and other similar modifications of the main argument are of *some* importance, they are rarely of *enough* quantitative importance to make a great deal of difference.

As a final proof of the correctness of my argument, I can point to the results of the two great recent attempts to apply the Labour doctrines of higher wages and shorter hours—the American experiment made in 1933 and the French experiment made in 1936. Between the middle and the end of 1933 hourly wage-rates in American industry were raised, by the operation of the National Industrial Recovery Act, by something like 18 per cent. The rapid and promising recovery movement of the early summer of 1933 came to an end, and throughout 1934 and 1935 recovery in American industry was very slow and inadequate. Of course, this may have been a coincidence ; but it is surely significant that the smallest degree of recovery was shown precisely where it could be expected if the argument of this chapter is sound—namely, in the industries making capital goods and construction materials. It is a matter of unanimous testimony by almost all observers that the inadequate volume of construction work was due to the inadequate margin of profit in many industries—and this, in turn, can be ascribed to the high rates of hourly wages imposed by the N.R.A. Nor did the workers benefit very much. By the middle of 1936 their *hourly* wage-rates were higher than they had been in 1929, before the depression. But their average weekly earnings—the money they had to spend—were 20 per cent. lower than in 1929. Moreover, unemployment was rife. Nobody can say for certain what would have happened if hourly wage-rates had not been pushed up so rapidly in 1933. But it is at least probable that there would have been a more rapid expansion both in employment and in workers' incomes. It is certain that in England, where there was no comparable increase in *wage-rates*, the increase in *wages* (*i.e.* the cash income of the workers) was far more rapid than in the United States.

In France, the effects of the Labour policies as regards wages and hours can only with difficulty be disentangled from the many other factors that have been at work during the last few years. But I do not think anybody can examine the record of these years with any attempt to forget a preconceived bias without coming to the conclusion that the *time* at which, and the *extent* to which, French Labour's demands were enforced were the chief of the reasons for the fact that France, alone of all the great nations, passed from one depression into another without any intervening period of prosperity. (Note that it was the timing and the extreme character of the demands that were to blame, rather than the demands themselves, for there cannot be any doubt that the French working-class had a great leeway of social progress to make up when the Socialists came into office in June 1936.) It is particularly instructive to notice how the tendencies of French trade were affected by the Labour programme. The first effect of M. Blum's assumption of office was a considerable increase in wage-rates (by between 15 per cent. and 20 per cent. on the average). This was too sudden a blow for French industry, and production accordingly declined between June and September 1936. Then the value of the franc was lowered in September, assisting prices to rise, enabling the profit-earners to get a little of their own back, and incidentally cancelling out a large part of the gain to the workers of the increase in wages. From October 1936 to March 1937 industrial recovery proceeded in France. Then the forty-hour week began to be strictly applied, causing still further increases in costs of production and choking off profits. Recovery was impeded again, and did not get another chance.

Both in France and in America the workers were naturally disappointed because the increase in wage-rates led to no increase in wages. Disappointed and indignant ; for, of course, it is hardly in human nature to admit that one's own policies have been mistaken. If the experiment misfired, it must have been due to some dirty trick by the other side. Both in France and in America there were loud complaints that the failure of the Labour experiments was due to a " strike of capital." Now, if by this it was meant to imply that capitalists were deliberately refraining from using their capital *solely* or *mainly* in order to embarrass a government they disliked, the accusation is nine parts nonsense. There are very few capitalists so Machiavellian or so consumed with political hatred that they will deliberately destroy half their fortunes in order to get rid of an obnoxious government. But if the accusation means that capitalists were genuinely — though perhaps mistakenly — afraid that it was not safe to invest capital in industrial enterprise, then, of course, there was a strike of capital in both countries. And why not ? The Labour people themselves are the first to proclaim the sacred right to strike in defence of injured interests. Why not for capitalists too ? And if a capitalist is honestly convinced that his money will be safer in a bank or a gilt-edged bond than it will be invested in a new factory, then shouting at him will not make him change his mind.

Let me repeat—this is not a moral argument. There is no ethical judgment of right or wrong. But so long as there is any element of freedom and judgment in the investing of capital, any process of discriminating between the more and the less profitable, the more and the less useful, we must be prepared for " strikes of capital." And those who make the investment of capital unattractive must not be surprised if no capital is invested.

They must not be surprised even when the resulting depression leads to the overthrow of rash Labour Governments.

6

Let us find room for a brief summation of the case on familiar lines.

Is Labour's policy good for Efficiency ? On the whole, No. The tendency of the trade union hierarchy to sympathize with the Conservative plan for turning every industry into a monopoly is, of course, subject to the same criticism as was expressed in the last chapter. Furthermore, Labour insistence on shortening hours, often without a full realization of the consequences, tends to make the productivity of the economic system less than the community would wish it to be if it were in full possession and had a full understanding of the facts.

Is Labour's policy good for Equity ? In intention, excellent. Indeed, the desire for greater equality of incomes is the mainspring of the whole movement. In effect, too, the existence of a Labour movement undoubtedly assists in the slow and gradual reduction of inequalities. We must give it a good mark under this head.

Is Labour's policy good for Regularity and Adaptability ? Unquestionably not. Labour shows a tendency to put forward its most sweeping demands for higher wages and shorter hours at precisely the wrong times. Partly this is because there is naturally more dissatisfaction with the working of the economic system in slump times than in boom times, with the result that left-wing governments are more common in depression times than when the " capitalist economy " appears to be working fairly well. Partly it is because the Labour movement has got so firmly into its head the theory (in my opinion quite wrong) that depressions are caused by unduly low wage-rates, that it advocates higher wage-rates as a *cure* for depressions. In point of fact, the right time to raise wages and shorten hours is when industry is prosperous ; depression time is the one time when it is certainly wrong.

A last word is necessary. Labour economics has been severely criticized in this chapter. But, of course, that does not in the least mean that I consider high wages or short hours as being bad in themselves. Very far from it. It is in no way the *intentions* of the Labour pro-gramme that are open to criticism, not even its *methods,* if they were likely to succeed, but merely its *chances of success.* I believe passionately that the little man, the forgotten man, the humble poor man has a right to a larger slice of the cake of material wealth—a larger slice and more leisure in which to consume it. I insist only that he will do himself no good if, in grabbing for a larger slice, he succeeds in shrinking the cake.

PART THREE.—SIGNPOSTS

Chapter VI

FROM ATTACK TO DEFENCE

THIS third part of this book is much the most difficult to write. If you have agreed with me up to this point, this is where you begin to be disappointed. If you have disagreed, this is where you begin to get your own back. It is not a very difficult task to define, in rotund generalities, what we want; that was Part One. It is a comparatively easy task to criticize the mistakes of others, with all the advantages of hindsight and of detachment from the busy pressure of human interests that rules the actual world; that was Part Two. But now we must begin to say what practical steps we would take if we had the power and the responsibility.

It is as well to make it clear from the start that no attempt will be made here to present a complete and coherent plan for solving all our economic woes. For one thing, there is no room in the final third of a very short book to sketch such a plan even in the barest outlines. And for another thing, all such complete and coherent plans are a vanity of the human spirit. I do not believe that you can get the body economic to rights with a single magic formula or a box of patent ideological pills any more than you can bring health to the human body by patent medicines. Good health results from following no theory to excess, and the curing of ill health is a matter of skilful doctoring in which the one fatal mistake is to have rigid ideas. The successful political economist, like the successful physician, is an artist almost more than a scientist. Improvisation is a necessary part of his art ; and the golden rule is to remember that circumstances always alter cases.

It is, of course, very inconvenient not to have a single formula to solve all difficult problems. But the inconvenience must be faced. Even with all the pages of an encyclopædia at our disposal, we could do no more than erect a few signposts for economic policy, a collection of guiding principles to help us in the future. And since we have only eighty short pages left, we can do no more than select a few of these signposts.

The watchword of this book is the three-fold slogan of Efficiency, Equity, Adaptability. Let us take it up once more, and see what can be done to advance towards each goal.

CHAPTER VII

ROADS TO ABUNDANCE

I

THE first problem that any economic policy has to solve is to increase the production of material wealth. It is perhaps no greater a problem than the equitable distribution of wealth or the maintenance of regularity in its output. But, by the same token, it is no less. It is essential once again to insist that the world does not now produce enough wealth to satisfy even the basic and essential needs of its inhabitants—that even a comparatively wealthy country like Great Britain could not now produce, even if every able-bodied man and woman were employed in useful work, all that its people want. There might be no starvation, but plenty of malnutrition. No nakedness, but plenty of shabbiness. No deaths from exposure, but plenty of slums.

This is the chief reason why we shall do well to insist on pushing ahead with the production of wealth—because despite all the facile clap-trap, the problem of production is manifestly not solved. But a second reason for insistence is precisely this clap-trap. The misleading slogan has been repeated so often that it has come to be believed. Because some foods occasionally rot without being consumed, because coffee is burned in Brazil, and herrings thrown back into the sea in England, because there is unemployment, people rush to the conclusion that we can already produce all we want, and that we need concern ourselves only with consuming it. In point of fact, surfeits of particular commodities were familiar to our ancestors. There is a reference in *Macbeth* to a farmer who " hanged himself in the expectation of plenty "—and unemployment was equally familiar to the Elizabethans (the Poor Law of 1601 was the first Unemployment Act). Yet nobody in his senses would argue that the Elizabethans had solved the problem of production. One of the first essentials of a sound economic policy is to recognize that while increased consumption is the *end* of policy, increased production must be its *means*.

Every one of us is a consumer. But almost every one of us is also either a producer or a member of a producer's family. Now the consumer and the producer have opposing interests. The consumer wants to have as much as possible to consume at the lowest possible prices. But the producer's interest is to maintain the scarcity value of what he produces—to restrict its quantity, and increase its price relatively to other prices. Each one of us is subject to this duality of interest ; we all want one particular price to be high, but all other prices to be low—and each of us means a different particular price. Many of the weaknesses of the Conservative and Labour policies discussed in the last two chapters arise from the fact that they are producers' policies. Let us suppose you are a consumer and a baker at the same time. It is your interest to see that the price of bread is high, but that the price of everything else is low. If you can attain that double objective, well and good. If you have to choose between the two, you will probably put your interests as a baker, *i.e.* your producer's interests, first. But if everybody puts their producers' interests first, every commodity will have some body of producers trying to enhance its scarcity value. Some will succeed; others will fail. But the nearer we get to a producer's paradise, the worse it will be for consumers. We shall lose as consumers all, and more than all, that we shall gain as producers. A man's producer-interest is closer to his mind. It affects his job and his income, and that seems much more important than the price of bread and sugar. A man is conscious of himself as a baker or a boilermaker; it is what sets him off from other men and gives him interests to defend against the community. He can hardly recognize himself at all as a consumer. Nevertheless, it is his consumer-interest that is fundamental, for the purpose of all work is to consume, and it is little profit to a man to have higher wages if they buy less bread. An individual group of producers may gain by making its product scarce; but only on the condition that all other producers' groups are not simultaneously making *their* products scarce. For if everything is made scarce we shall all be worse off, however much our nominal wage-rates or our nominal profits have been swollen. There is thus a grave risk that when the dominant political parties are based upon confederations of producers—be they business men or wage-earners—they will pursue a producers' policy to the detriment of their own real interests.

Since the consumer-interest, though less consciously felt, is more fundamental than the producer-interest, it might be assumed that an economic policy that exalted the consumer would be the ideal. The old classical theory of *laisser-faire* was just such a system. The theory, in its full rigour, was that a régime of unrestricted competition between all individuals would automatically accomplish the miracle of reconciling divergent individual interests with the interest of the community. Nobody should be allowed either to buy or to sell anything except in open unrestricted competition. If each individual were compelled to compete, both in earning his living and in spending it, with a large number of other individuals as anxious as he himself to drive a good bargain, their competition would, it was claimed, automatically ensure that each got his deserts. Workmen freely competing for work would drive down wages to a sum exactly equal to the value of their work ; manufacturers competing for a market would drive down the price of goods to exactly their cost of production *plus* only the necessary minimum of profit. And since free competition excludes, by definition, any artificial restriction of production and supply, a system such as this ensures the maximum possible production of goods. The application of the principle might impose very severe hardships on some sections of the community who were pinched out by competition. But their loss was the means of a far greater gain for the community. Their sufferings were unfortunate, but any attempt to impede the free working of competition would impose even greater loss on the community. This magic effect of competition was the Hidden Hand, a divinely appointed and universally applicable device for ensuring that individual self-seeking was miraculously transmuted into mutual benefit. It was at once the explanation and the justification for our grandfathers' fanatical belief in *laisser-faire*, in letting things alone ; if there were, in reality, such a beneficent and effective principle at work, it was not merely possible, but necessary, to leave it quite free to do its work.

We can, of course, see clearly to-day that the unexpressed assumptions upon which this doctrine was built never had much validity, and have even less to-day. Men are not in a position to compete on equal terms ; the rich man always has an advantage over the poor. Secondly, natural and institutional factors are constantly preventing free competition, as when Nature makes one coal mine richer than another, or the state grants a patent for some essential process. But either unequal bargaining power or monopoly upsets the theory of the Hidden Hand. In the world as it is actually constituted, unrestricted free competition would not result in an automatic distribution of economic benefits among individuals according to their deserts ; it would be a perpetuation of inequalities, an establishment of injustice.

For these reasons, the world has turned its back on *laisser-faire*. But in doing so, it has tended to overlook the great advantage of *laisser-faire* : that it does prevent any restriction of production, and thus makes for the maximum Efficiency of the economic system, whatever may be its effect on Equity and Regularity. In our search for means of increasing Efficiency, should we exhort the world to turn back to *laisser-faire*, to raise free competition once more to its throne ?

We can save ourselves the trouble of arguing this point. For any such return to *laisser-faire* is plainly impossible. True, there are many who preach it (most of them people in strong bargaining positions, who would do pretty well out of free competition). But one needs only to reflect that such a policy would require the abolition of trade unions (or at least of the doctrine of standard wages and collective bargaining), the "unscrambling" of the large amalgamations that dominate so many industries, and the abandonment of all attempts by Government to help particular industries, to see how impossible it would be. People will not do those things. Doubtless they *ought* to think of themselves first and foremost as consumers. Doubtless they *ought* to be more concerned with the price of bread and sugar and milk and tea and all the other consumable necessaries of life than with their rate of wages. Perhaps they *ought* to realize that a régime of free competition (with proper safeguards against abuse) might do them more good in their rôle as consumers than harm in their rôle as producers. But, in fact, people do not think that way, and any realistic economic policy must recognize the fact.

There is thus no chance of Efficiency being guaranteed by free competition under a system of *laisser-faire*, or of our destinies being once more entrusted to the Hidden Hand. But though we reject *laisser-faire*, though we have discovered that the Hidden Hand has an array of hidden jokers up its sleeve, we shall be making a very great mistake if we ignore completely the interests of the consumer. A pure producers' policy leads straight to restriction and poverty, since each producer's quickest way to wealth is to seek means to make the community poorer. If free competition is not to be our watchword, we must find other ways of reconciling the individual interest with the collective welfare, for it is only when such a reconciliation has been achieved that the economic system will pour forth its maximum production of material wealth.

Our task, then, is to assume, as realists, that the dominant forms of economic organization will be producers' units, but to seek means of ensuring that this world of producers shall act as if it had the consumer's interest at heart. And since the more we all become conscious of our separate and separatist interests as producers, the more anonymous and inarticulate we become as consumers, it is increasingly important that the state, the community itself, should be the tribune of the consumer. As economics comes more and more to dominate politics, it becomes the supreme task of political science to find a mechanism by which the Whole can be represented as strongly as the Parts.

2

Within the framework of this sort of society, what can we do to ensure a maximum production of goods and services for consumption?

Quite a great deal can be done merely by recognizing the necessity for pushing ahead with production. The old-fashioned gospel of hard work has rather gone out of fashion in the democratic countries in recent years. This has been due, I think, to the combination of four factors. First, there is the fact that, though we have not yet arrived at the goal of sufficiency for all, we have, in the Western democracies, for the first time in human history, come within sight of it. It is a very human failing to slacken the pace when the goal comes in sight. Second, within our lifetime there has been a very considerable reduction in the average hours of work without any perceptible diminution in the average standard of living ; and this naturally leads to the belief that work is not necessary. Third, the growth of the Labour movement and the spread of theories that encourage the worker to believe that endless riches are within his grasp if he will end his " exploitation " by the capitalist, lead to big demands being put forward for more wages in return for less work, in the belief that " it will come out of profits." And finally, the chronic economic disease of unemployment makes it hard to believe that there can be a shortage of labour.

There is something in each of these arguments, and a great deal in some of them. But in combination they have been greatly overdone, and the idiotic belief is now widespread that, in some magic way, the less work is done the richer everybody will be. This comes out most clearly in the agitation for the reduction of working hours, which was fully examined in Chapter V.

It will be an immense gain to our economic policy if we can see this matter clearly ; if we can realize that we can have more leisure if we want it, or more income, but that we can hardly have much of both together. There is a great deal of sound realistic sense in the old-fashioned gospel of hard work, and it is time that it came back to fashion. It is no longer as true as it used to be that man lives by the sweat of his brow. Work done is no longer to be measured by foot-pounds of sheer energy, or even by man-hours of presence on the job. But it remains eternally true that we can consume only what we produce, and that every form of production involves human labour. The authoritarian states preach a doctrine of work—work for that Moloch, the state. The democracies need a similar doctrine of work for the wealth of the community of individual citizens.

The homily need not, however, be confined to Labour.

There are many other examples in latter-day economics of the failure to recognize the elementary truth that the community cannot be enriched by a restriction of the production of wealth. Business men have developed, with matchless ingenuity, an astonishing array of devices for restriction. Apart from the direct limitation of output which a monopolist may decree, or a producers' association may impose upon its members, there are such expedients as the fixation of minimum prices, the exclusion of competitors by customs tariffs and quotas, or even—in some trades—a complete prohibition upon any new entrant to the trade. In the United States, all these devices (except the customs tariff), broadly speaking, are illegal. Should we make them illegal here?

For a variety of reasons, the complete legal prohibition of restrictionist devices is not sound policy, especially for a country like Britain which is no longer expanding in size. The great majority of restrictions on production, it is true, are imposed merely to defend the excessive profits or security of some vested interest. They render no service to the community, and frequently do it harm by withholding goods from consumption. Thus, if there were not a monopoly in the sale of milk, which keeps up the price, it is almost certain that more milk would be drunk. And whatever effect that might have upon the farmers or the dairymen, it would be an advantage to the community. Restrictionism which merely serves private ends deserves to be condemned.

But there are cases where some restriction of output is in the general interest. For example, there are many industries in which either the demand for the product or the supply of it varies very greatly from time to time.

Variations of demand are familiar in many industries, especially those which make capital goods. Great variations of supply are most frequent in the agricultural and raw material industries. In some cases, such as wheat, the size of any particular year's crop is not due to anybody's rational judgment, or even to the combined effect of the reaction of millions of individual producers to a given set of circumstances, but to a sheer accident of Nature. If there is a big crop of wheat this year, that is not because there was a shortage of wheat last year, which wheat producers have taken steps to remedy; there may have been an equal surplus last year. Or in other raw material industries—such as rubber, for instance—where the size of the available output is (as it is not in the case of wheat) the result of conscious human decision, the time between the making of the decision and its maturing is so long that no rational judgments are possible. Thus it is five years after a rubber tree is planted before it bears, and whatever may have been the reasons for planting it in the first place, they are likely to be the wrong reasons five years later. In industries of this sort, where either demand or supply, or both, fluctuate violently, it is perfect nonsense to talk about a natural adjustment of the one to the other. If left to themselves, these industries will be wildly prosperous in some years, bitterly depressed in others—and in either condition they are doing no good to the community. There is everything to be said, in these cases, for instituting an artificial control of the quantity of the commodity coming on to the market, and for making the best possible attempt to bring supply and demand into adjustment. And it is hardly a valid objection to such a system that it results in a restriction of supply in some years.

Between 1925 and 1932, the price of rubber fluctuated between 4s. 7d. and 1¾d. a lb. Everybody—rubber growers, rubber users, and the community—would have been better served if it had been possible to keep the price steady at, say, 1s. a lb., even though in 1932 the maintenance of a price of 1s. would have meant a smaller consumption of rubber than the actual price of 1¾d. a lb. This form of restriction, then, is justifiable—*provided* that it is pure equalization between good and bad years, and that there is no restriction at all on the average over a period of years. This proviso is all-important ; in the past, most such control schemes have been put in the hands of the producers, who have used them, as was only natural, to keep the price higher than can be justified on the average, and thus restricting production and consumption below what could have been expected on the average. If abused in this way, control schemes become mere instruments of private rapacity, and the community would be better off without them, even if their abandonment meant a return to violent swings of price. But some of the newer control schemes are more reasonable, and they try to maintain an average price that is reasonable for the consumer as well as for the producer.

Restriction can also be justified in the case of an industry that is suffering from a permanent excess of productive capacity. Thus in 1939 there were more coal miners and coal mines in Great Britain than were conceivably likely to be wanted. The world can produce far more sugar than it requires. The Lancashire cotton industry will never again have a market for all the cotton cloth it is equipped to produce. Since we have reached the stage when our population has ceased to increase, and we shall soon reach the beginning of the inevitable decline, problems of over-capacity are likely to be considerably more frequent in the future than they have been in the past. Now, if an overcrowded industry is allowed to go on with unrestricted free competition, its struggles to find a market will lead to such fierce cutthroat competition that, after a time, nobody will make a profit at all. Wages will be reduced and the industry will find it impossible to raise the money to keep its capital equipment up-to-date or even reasonably efficient. The theory of *laisser-faire* is that, in such conditions, the weaker firms go bankrupt and drop out, until the industry is reduced to the size that can just cope with the demand. In actual fact, however, if this happens at all, it happens only with agonizing slowness. When a cotton-mill goes bankrupt, it rarely goes out of business ; it is more often bought up cheap and goes on competing more fiercely than ever.

When an industry has got into this state, free competition is no remedy for its troubles. The public, it is true, gets its goods very cheaply—but only at the cost of slowly consuming some of the valuable fixed capital which enriches the community. If an industry is of value to the community, it is worth the community's while to pay whatever price for its goods is necessary to maintain it in good working order. But with chronic over-capacity, this is not what happens ; and the community will one day pay the price for its cheap supplies when it finds itself with a completely derelict industry on its hands, requiring very heavy expenditure of new capital to restore its workability. In these circumstances, also, some restriction of output is in the community's interest —provided, once more, it is not abused to provide an excessive rate of profit for private monopolies. We can add a further proviso—that if there is excess productive capacity in an industry and the community agrees as a result to some form of restriction of output, the community has the right to insist that the most efficient plant shall be worked to the full and the least efficient plant not at all. Restriction schemes should be planned in the general interest, not as pension schemes for elderly factories.

It is possible, then, to build up quite a good case for limitation of production in certain instances. Indeed, when we come to the era of shrinking population, they may even cease to be exceptional cases, and we may have to have a general policy of limitation—though hardly of restriction—to ensure an orderly retreat. But we are a good way from that stage yet, and for the present we ought to have a healthy bias against all forms of restriction of output. Whenever a restriction scheme is put forward, the onus should be put upon its advocates of proving that it will be in the general interest—and in the process of proof every argument to the effect that it will be in the interests of the applicant producers should be rigorously excluded. *Of course*, restriction of supply is in the interest of producers, and all producers are deserving. There is a regrettable tendency nowadays to think that if the restriction of production of, say, milk would benefit the dairy farmers (who, on the average, are poor men) that is sufficient reason for agreeing to it. The state, while admitting that there are exceptions in which some restriction of supply may be advantageous, should lean over backwards in its determination to establish that the particular example of restrictionism that is being advocated is, in fact, the

exceptional case, from which the community, as well as
the producer, would derive advantage. And, as a general
principle, nobody should be allowed to enlist the compulsive powers of the state to enforce any form of
restriction, without admitting the community to a share
—in most cases the decisive share—in the management
of the restriction scheme.

3

So far, in our search for the means of increasing
production, we have, in the main, merely expounded
negative maxims. It has been suggested, in the first
place, that we ought to reinstate the doctrine that work is
the origin of wealth, that consumption can come only
after production, and that we ought to abandon such
mistaken policies of deliberately diminishing the possibilities of production as spring from the fallacy that
" the problem of production has been solved." Secondly,
as a particular example of this general principle, it has
been suggested that the state ought not to lend its
assistance to any scheme for a restriction of supply until it
is completely satisfied that not merely the producers but
the community as a whole would benefit.

Now, even if we stopped at this point, the result of this
chapter would not be quite as negative as appears. There
is an inherent tendency in the modern economic system
for the productivity of human labour to increase. In
fact, the rate of increase is remarkably consistent over
long periods of time. So far as we can tell, the average
rate of increase of productivity throughout the nineteenth century was something between $\frac{3}{4}$ per cent. and
$1\frac{1}{4}$ per cent.—let us say 1 per cent.—per annum. That is

to say that, on the average, Man was able each year to produce about 1 per cent. more wealth in a day's labour than in the previous year. And, again, so far as we can tell, that rate of progress still holds good. Now 1 per cent. per annum compound is not particularly rapid—it involves doubling only every seventy years—but at least it is a steady rate of progress which appears to be largely automatic under *laisser-faire* or controlled economy. The least that deliberate economic policy can do is to see that this underlying tendency is not obstructed.

Is there, however, nothing we can do to speed up the 1 per cent. per annum ? If we could turn it into 2 per cent. per annum, the productivity of the average man—which, in the long run, is exactly the same thing as his standard of living—would double every generation. Is there nothing positive that can be done ?

Before we start to look for an answer to this question, there is a distinction to be drawn. One way to increase the output of the community is to see that everybody who is ready to work is given a job to do—in other words, to solve the problem of unemployment. This is the problem with which we shall be concerned in Chapter X. But it is not the problem with which we are concerned in this chapter. Let us suppose that we have succeeded in reducing the unemployment percentage from its 1939 level of, say, 12 per cent. to 4 per cent., which is about the lowest figure that could conceivably be maintained for a long period. Employment would have risen from 88 per cent. to 96 per cent., and there would have been an increase in production of approximately one-eleventh. But once that had been done, there would be no further progress unless the productivity of each member of the 96 per cent. went on increasing. In just the same way, a community whose unemployment proportion remained obstinately at the high figure of 20 per cent., might nevertheless continue to make slow progress if the productivity of the remaining 80 per cent. went on rising. There are, therefore, two separate problems— the abolition of unemployment and the increase of productivity *per worker in work*. In point of fact, it is quite probable that the solution of each problem is to be found along very much the same lines. But that need not affect the fact that we are here concerned with the second problem only.

A necessary preliminary to inquiring what can be done to increase the rate of progress is to investigate what brings it into existence in the first place. How is it that each year, on the average, an hour's labour produces about 1 per cent. more wealth than in the year before ? It would be flattering to assume that we are, each year, 1 per cent. cleverer or more skilful than before. But there is very little evidence to support such a belief. Human cleverness should show itself most conspicuously in inventions. But it is very difficult to believe that the flow of inventions comes with such astonishing regularity that their fruits mature at the rate of 1 per cent. per annum. (Perhaps that is carrying it too far ; for the process is probably not quite regular from year to year. But if we say 10 per cent. per decade we shall be quite safely within the bounds of accuracy, and we shall still have established the impressive regularity of the rate of material progress). Some inventions are manifestly much more important than others ; and major inventions seem to come in groups rather than in a regular progress. If material progress depended solely on the supply of inventions, we should expect it to go in fits and starts, not regularly.

Yet, inventions and inventiveness obviously have a great deal to do with it. We can establish that fact by observing that the rate of material progress has been faster in the last two centuries, since Man started to bring machinery to his assistance in producing goods, than it appears to have been before. What appears to be the truth is that it is not the *discovery* of new technical processes that creates material progress, but their *application*. Application is necessarily a gradual process, for it requires the investment of capital, of which there is only a limited supply, since its only source is in the savings of the community. The limiting factor in the rate of progress is thus not the supply of inventions, but the supply of capital. Even if all invention stopped over-night, we could go on for quite a time increasing the average productivity of labour by spreading the application of the existing inventions. But if the investment of capital suddenly ceased, the inventors could all work overtime without their labours having any effect on the output of wealth.

The importance of the investment of capital for the rate of progress can be very clearly illustrated by examining a few cases of notably rapid progress. The outstanding example is probably the United States. When North America was first settled, the standard of living of its inhabitants was probably lower than that of the countries they had come from. It was probably still below the English standard a century ago, possibly even later. Why is it that the United States has succeeded in building up a higher standard of living for its inhabitants than any other country? It cannot be the mere size of the country—the number of acres of useful land per head of the population—because if it were, the American standard of living would be shared by Russia, Argentina, and Brazil. Nor can it be the mineral wealth of the country, for other countries have almost the same variety (Russia) or richness (Malaya) of natural resources. It cannot be, as is often argued, the size of the market provided by 125 million people living within one customs barrier, for these conditions are reproduced in India and China. What is unique in the United States is that every pair of working hands is assisted by more horse-power of machinery there than anywhere else. And this formidable total of machinery has been accumulated because, decade by decade, the amount of new capital invested in the United States has formed a higher proportion of the total national income than in other countries.

If you ask why there has been such a heavy investment of capital in the United States, the answer is manifold. But the largest element in it is, undoubtedly, that the return on the investment of capital there has been higher than elsewhere. It is fully possible, however, to provide other examples of the fertilizing effects of capital invest- ment in other countries where the rate of return is of less importance. Russia has shown, in the last two decades, a higher rate of progress in the production of many (though not all) of the forms of industrial wealth than most other countries. The explanation is to be found, not in the inherent excellence of the Communist theory, but in the fact that the Soviet dictatorship has been able to impose on the Russian people a high rate of saving (*i.e.* a low proportion of consumption to total output) and hence a high proportion of capital investment to total income. There are few better examples of the virtues of capital than the Communist experiment—I mean, of course, the virtues of having a great volume of capital to invest, and not the virtues of the system by which the greater part of the capital is privately owned. It is the volume of capital, not its ownership, that is fundamental to economic progress, as is shown by the fact that our two examples have been drawn impartially from Capitalist America and Communist Russia.

This analysis would suggest that the main essential for an increased rate of progress would be an increased rate of investment of capital. But before we leap to that conclusion there is one obvious question that we must ask. America is—or at least was until recently—a young and developing country. Russia is manifestly under-equipped. Both countries still have rapidly rising populations. There is an obvious *demand* for capital in both countries. But do the American and Russian arguments apply to a nation like Great Britain—old, crowded, and nearly stationary in size ? Clearly, the arguments *have* applied to Great Britain in the past, for we have shown a higher rate of progress over a longer period than almost every other country. But will they apply in the future ?

The fact that we are ceasing to grow in population obviously tends to lessen the demand for capital. In a growing country, part of each year's investment of capital is required merely to provide an increase in the existing mechanical equipment to match the increase in the working population. It increases the *total* productivity of the country, but it only maintains the *average* productivity of each worker, which is what determines the rate of progress ; only what remains of the annual supply of capital is available for this more valuable purpose. In a country that is not growing, the whole annual supply of savings has to find employment in providing new additional capital. The demand for savings, relatively to the supply, is smaller, and accordingly, the average return on invested savings is lower. But notice what this means. It does not mean that there is a fixed amount of capital that can be invested each year, and no more. There is, in every country, an infinite supply of ways of investing capital to produce *some* return in increased productivity. But naturally those that promise the biggest return are invested in first. The available supply of capital will go first to those projects that promise a return of 10 per cent., next to those that promise to yield 9 per cent., and so forth. An old country will be able to invest just as large a proportion of its income every year as a new country, and it will derive some economic benefit from it. But the average return of economic benefit per £100 of capital invested will be lower. A new country investing each year, say, one-tenth of its total income, will secure as a result a larger rate of progress than an old country investing the same proportion.

But the really essential point is this : that every country, new or old, will progress more rapidly if it saves and usefully invests a relatively large proportion of its national income, than if the same country only saves and invests a smaller proportion of its national income.

The answer to the main question of this chapter is, then, the investment of capital. And how are we to secure a greater investment of capital ? There is comparatively little difficulty in providing the capital to invest. Indeed, as will be argued in Chapter IX., we are threatened in the present century with the chronic recurrence of an over-supply of savings, *i.e.* of more money being saved than is being invested. Moreover, successful investment, by increasing wealth, produces its own supply of savings. The problem is to secure that all the money that is saved is invested in such a way as to increase the wealth-producing capacity of the community. This is where we come back to the importance of profits ; for profits are both the sign that capital has been properly invested (unless the profits emerge from monopoly extortion) and the attraction to capital waiting for investment. Now this does not mean (as will appear in the next paragraph) that profits must be kept at an excessive level ; nor does it mean (as will appear in Chapter IX.) that profits must continue to serve as the main aliment of an idle rich class. But it does mean (so long as there is any economic and personal freedom left) that a steady and abundant flow of capital into industry cannot be secured in a community which follows the Labour doctrine that the worker can produce less and still consume more by " taking it out of profits." It is worth repeating once more that a policy that wished to increase the standard of living of the working class as rapidly as possible would take as its first practical objective the maintenance of profits at a fair average level.

The second requisite for an abundant flow of capital into investment is that investors should not be encouraged to expect too high a return. There is never a shortage of possibilities of investing capital to give a return ; but there is frequently a shortage of possibilities of investing to get a return of 10 per cent. per annum ; and if investors are encouraged to believe that anything below 10 per cent., or 8 per cent., or 6 per cent. is not worth while, investment will not be undertaken and savings will rot in idleness. If it is true that the average return on capital is going to be lower in England in future than in the past, this point becomes doubly important. In the technical phrase, the problem is one of reducing the average rate of interest that is earned, or expected to be earned, on invested capital. How that can be done is a technical and complex problem of monetary management on which I do not propose to enter here. But it can be done; and the policy of the state towards its National Debt, and of the Bank of England towards the Money Market, can both exert a powerful influence. For if a man who has saved money is not attracted to invest it in industry, he will either deposit it at interest in some financial institution or buy gilt-edged Government bonds. And the higher the rate of interest he can get in these ways, the higher the average rate of return on industrial investment will have to be to tempt him. On the other hand, a low Bank Rate (which determines other rates in the Money Market) and a low yield on gilt-edged securities will make him more ready to invest in industry. And what applies to the individual saver applies with even more force to the institutions which will have to do our saving for us if we abolish the individual rich man.

The motto for a steady and abundant flow of capital into investment—the slogan for a rapid rate of material progress—must therefore be " Low Profits but plenty of them." The rest will follow.

But the rest will not follow quite automatically. It is of no use having an increased flow of capital into industry if, when it is transmuted into productive equipment, it is held idle by a policy of restriction and monopoly. Such a policy may increase the yield on a small part of the investment of capital, but only at the cost of reducing the quantity that can be invested. So much has been written on policies of restriction in this and preceding chapters that no more need be said here on the general issue.

There is, however, a particular application of restriction which is all the more pernicious for being unconscious. Machinery—that is, capital—shows its highest virtues when it is used for what have come to be known as mass-production methods. Now the mass-production article, just because it is mass-produced, has to be sold very cheaply ; the ratio of profit must be very low. But the machinery is used so intensively that the yield on the capital invested may be quite high. " Low profits and quick turnover " has been the secret of many of the largest fortunes. Henry Ford was the archetype of all mass-producers. Now it would have been quite open to Ford, during the crucial stage of his career, to have decided to produce expensive cars with a high rate of profit instead of cheap cars with a low rate of profit on each. Nobody would have accused him of being a restrictionist if he had so decided. Indeed, nobody would ever have known that a cheap car was possible— just as nobody knew just how cheaply shoes could be made until M. Bat'a showed the world. The point is that the mass-production methods required to produce a Ford car or a Bat'a shoe need a far higher proportion of machinery (capital) to labour than the Rolls-Royce or the expensive shoe.

But that is not the whole of the secret. For Ford might have discovered means of making a car for a third of the previous price. But if, as a result, he sold only three times as many cars, he would have gone bankrupt, because his output would not have been large enough to keep his machinery busy. His genius—or his good luck—was that by cutting the price in three, he multiplied sales by ten or twenty. In the technical term, the demand for cars is (or was at that time) *elastic*, and a reduction in price produced a more than proportionate increase in production. Now clearly, the investment of capital will bring far higher returns, to the investor and to the community, if it is used to cheapen a product for which there is an elastic demand than if it is used to produce more of a product for which the demand is inelastic (*e.g.* bread ; if the price of bread were cut in half, the probability is that less than twice as much would be eaten). But this sort of investment requires a high degree of individual courage. It involves the spending of large sums of money on expensive machinery in the faith, not merely that the resulting lower prices will lead to increased sales, but that the increase in demand will be greater than the reduction in cost. The guess may be wrong, and in that case the money is lost. If it is right, it is the most profitable and beneficent of all methods of investing capital.

But the risks are so great that they have to be taken by individuals. All the great mass-production discoveries are associated with the names of individuals—Ford and Woolworth in America ; Morris and Austin and the mass-production clothiers, Burton and Price, in England ; Bat'a on the Continent—all these are one-man businesses. It would be extremely difficult to name a business that has been a pioneer in opening up a mass-production market that has not been dominated by one man. Boards and committees, operating with other people's money, can supply judgment and administrative ability ; but imaginative courage is not their long suit.

Chapter VIII

PLANNING FOR PLENTY

In pure logic, there is no reason for beginning a new chapter at this point. For what we are now going to discuss is really only the last series of points that should be mentioned under the general heading of increasing the Efficiency of the economic system. But Chapter VII., if it were to include all this as a last section, would be of quite inordinate length.

We have hitherto been concerned with the main principles that ought to be followed if the production of wealth (which means the consumption of wealth) is to be raised to a maximum. We must keep the consumer's interests at heart. We must not encourage anything that would restrict the production of wealth, whether it be the fallacious doctrine that Labour can eat more by working less or the employer's temptation to restrict his output. And we must seek means to increase the flow of capital into investment in enterprise. But we also began the chapter by rejecting the doctrine that the best way to secure all these objects was to insist on free competition and then leave everybody to fight it out without interference. If we reject *laisser-faire* we accept some element of planning and organization. But what sort of planning or organization would come nearest to meeting the requirements that have been laid down in this chapter ?

I

One thing can be said emphatically at the outset about planning. If there is planning to be done, it must be done in the interests of the community as a whole. The community cannot afford to be more planned against than planning. This means that the central planning—the master-plan, as it were—must be done by the community itself. Stated as a principle, this seems obvious. But it is astonishing how little the principle is followed, and how little the state, as the embodiment of the community, has equipped itself for planning. The reason is probably to be found in the history of economic thought. Throughout the Victorian era and right up to our own days, the doctrine of *laisser-faire*, though modified in detail, was so dominant in economic teaching (as distinct from economic practice) that the whole apparatus of Government was built up to serve purely negative purposes of regulation. Most of our senior Civil Servants to this day are men who imbibed this doctrine at the feet of their *almæ matres* and cannot now get it out of their systems. The result is that the state, with all its resources, is less well equipped for the conscious formulation of long-term economic policies than many individual business concerns and most private trade associations.

Clearly the first requirement for a democratic economic policy must be the creation of adequate central planning machinery. Many people are frightened by this—it smacks to them of Sovietism. But that such an attitude is wholly unreasonable can be shown by two reflections. First, it is obviously desirable that if the state is going to intervene in the economic machine it should know what it is doing. Under any system of society, properly planned and balanced intervention will be better calculated to produce results than haphazard, improvised, makeshift devices that trip over each other's toes. Even if you dislike state intervention, it is a fantastic policy to oppose planning when the sole result of so doing is not to reduce the amount of state intervention (which mounts from year to year), but merely to secure that it is self-contradictory, amorphous, and inefficient. And secondly, the creation of planning machinery for the state does not in the least mean that the state will take over the running of all industry and commerce. Because there is a large and complicated signal-box at Waterloo Station, it does not follow that the signalmen drive all the trains, still less that they decide how many trains shall run to Southampton and how many to Portsmouth. The only reason for believing that *planned* state intervention is synonymous with *increased* state intervention is that with proper planning more of the experiments in state intervention might turn out to every one's satisfaction.

2

But perhaps increased intervention by the state is something to be hoped for ? That, at least, is the Socialist case. The devout Socialist looks forward to a time when every facet of economic activity will be under the control of public organizations. On the other hand, many people, even of those who accept the necessity for a considerable degree of state intervention, regard it as an evil necessity, and look upon each manifestation of it as the sign of some weakness in the national economy.

Which view is right ? The only realistic answer that can be given is that neither is right. There are some sorts of economic activity which it would be ruinous to submit to control. Some examples were given on page 148 of industries which would never have developed to their present size unless they had been led by bold individuals who were free to follow their faith and courage. To advocate " the nationalization of *all* the means of production, distribution, and supply " may fit into a tidy logical argument. But as a proposal for bringing to a maximum the power of the community to produce wealth it is nonsensical.

On the other hand, there are other forms of economic activity which need to be organized by the supreme authority of the state and others which need to be publicly owned. We should not wait for an industry to get into desperate straits under private enterprise before prescribing some form of state organization or ownership. Public control must not be regarded as a Home for Economic Incurables. We should regard it as perfectly natural that some healthy industries (such as the business of the Post Office) should be run by the state. And in deciding where to draw the line between those forms of activity which call for state intervention and those which do not, the only sensible attitude is to show no bias whatever on one side or on the other. It might be argued that since the state and its servants have had in the past, and still in some cases have to-day, a manifestly unreasonable bias *against* intervention, it would be as well for the rest of us to counteract this attitude by having a bias *in favour of* intervention. But it can also be argued that the interventionists tend to overlook the very great technical difficulty of finding enough competent men to put in charge of the state's experiments in economic organization. In my opinion, these arguments just about cancel each other out. The only wise policy is to approach each individual case without any prepossession whatever in favour either of leaving it as an open field for free competition, or of submitting it to some degree of enforced organization by the state.

We have to recognize, then, that there are some forms of economic activity that are best left alone and others that are naturally suited for state intervention. What sort of businesses fall into the latter classification ? There is no one identifying characteristic by which the industry that is ripe for state attention can be distinguished. In the following paragraphs six types are identified, but the list is not intended to be in the least complete :

1. The most obvious cases are those public services which, by general consent, should be run by the state or by public (*i.e.* non-profit making) bodies, because of the direct way in which they affect the interests of the state. In every country the business of the Post Office is run by the state. In most (but not in all) the telephones and telegraphs are also publicly owned. In Great Britain the business of broadcasting is run as a state-owned but autonomous concern, and most people who have experienced the alternative of advertising-controlled broadcasting would vote for the British system. These we may call Public Services.

2. There are many other services which affect the public interest very closely, though not quite so intimately as the first category. We may call these Public Utilities, and obvious examples are the provision of electricity and gas and the transport industry. A less obvious example is, or should be, the industry of

supplying the people with food. Most of these industries
are now in private ownership. But they obviously require close supervision by the community in their
operations, and with each one the question will constantly arise whether the community would not be better
served if the state were to take it over. In the case of the
Public Services, the answer to the question is emphatically
in favour of public ownership. In the case of the Public
Utilities, there is room for doubt. That is the distinction
between the two.

3. Some industries are in fact run as monopolies ; they
have fallen under the domination or the entire control of
one concern, or of a ring of co-operating concerns. In
these cases the community has to consider whether it is
being exploited by the private monopoly. When one
concern monopolizes an industry it is usually a large
concern, and therefore already subject to the evils of
bureaucratic administration. If so, handing over to the
state would involve no change of methods and might
save the community from exploitation. On the other
hand, it does not in the least follow that because a concern
dominates an industry it is in fact extorting monopoly
profits from the public. But every monopoly is naturally
under suspicion.

4. There are industries occupying vital key positions
in the economic machine which are notorious for sheer
technical inefficiency. The steel industry, before about
1935, was a case in point. Even now it does not seem
able to produce steel as cheaply as most, if not all, of its
major competitors in foreign countries. In cases of this
sort the community has a duty to ask itself whether it
could not achieve greater efficiency by imposing a
compulsory reorganization on the industry.

5. There are also industries which are suffering from permanent excess of productive capacity. The trouble in category 4 is that the industry is charging too much for its products. In category 5 the trouble is that the industry is selling too cheaply—too cheaply to save its personnel from poverty or to maintain its fixed capital. The argument for intervention here is compounded equally of the need to put the producers out of their misery and of the desire to protect the community from consuming its capital. It is in this category that state intervention is most familiar, because in these cases the producers themselves want it. There is the corresponding danger that it will be granted in their interests alone.

6. Finally, there are the industries—like beet sugar and civil aviation—which depend upon subsidies from the state for their existence. Obviously, they require close control, and in most cases it will be better for them to be run by frankly public bodies.

It would be fully possible to draw up a similar list of sorts of businesses which should *not* be subjected to state intervention. But it is enough for the moment to say that they would include all sorts of businesses where the emphasis is on pioneering rather than administration, on boldness and courage rather than on sagacity and soundness, on quick adaptation to changing circumstances rather than the deliberate exploitation of established principles. In general, this means that new industries should be left to themselves unless there is some overriding reason (as there is, for example, in the new industry of broadcasting) for the state to take a hand. And since there will always be new industries, the sensible man will refuse to look forward to a time, however remote, when *all* forms of business undertakings are in public hands. In developing a new industry, the private employer benefits the community much more than he costs it.

3

Once the choice has been made of those forms of business that are suitable for public attention, the question arises how the nature of the intervention is to be determined. On this there are two schools of thought. The Conservative, or business man's, principle is to let each industry plan its own organization and for the state to impose nothing that is not freely agreed to, or even asked for, by the business men already in possession of the field. The Socialist principle is to treat each industry selected for treatment as a prisoner of state, to deal with it kindly and justly but with all the compulsive power of an Act of Parliament. Both methods are equally objectionable. The former leads to the organization of industry being turned against the interests of the community. The latter leads, unless it is very carefully handled, to the expulsion from the industry of all those who know most about it.

Once again, the wise course seems to be to pick the best from the two opposing alternatives. From the Socialist side we must take the principle that it is for the community, after consulting its own interests, and not for any group of producers, to decide which industries are to be submitted to what form of public intervention or control. We must also adopt the social (if not the Socialist) principle that the object of such intervention or control is to serve the community, not the vested interests of any individual group. And from the Conservative side we must take the fact that the best people to run an industry are the people who are running it at present. To replace an intelligent and efficient business man by a bureaucrat or a board of elected mediocrities is to invite inefficiency. In very many cases the problem resolves itself into choosing the most able man at present in an industry and putting him in charge to run it on business principles.

From what has already been said in this section of the chapter, it must be abundantly clear that there is no single form of organization that will suit every business enterprise that the community brings under its wing. Each case requires its individual treatment, and the solutions will inevitably range all the way from running the business as a government department with a minister responsible to parliament (such as the Post Office), to running it as an ordinary limited company with one or two directors appointed by the Government. Endless discussion has been devoted to the best methods of organizing public enterprises, and it is not proposed to go over the ground again here. Indeed, excessive discussion of problems of organization has its dangers. What matters most is not the exact form of the constitution of an industry, but the way in which it goes to work. A private monopoly may, in fact, act better in the interests of the community than a nationalized Board (though the probability is against it). Just as you cannot make a man honest by Act of Parliament, so you cannot guarantee by even the most perfect legislation that an industry will be efficiently managed. This is the mistake made by all the people who devote large volumes to discussing the form that socialization should take without bothering about the sort of men who are to be appointed to run a socialized industry or the principles by which they are to be guided. Nevertheless, in spite of these disadvantages, inherent in any discussion of forms of individual government, it is worth while to point out a few dangers that are often overlooked.

Perhaps the most insidious danger is that of yielding to the specious pleas of what is called Industrial Democracy, or Industrial Self-Government. Every second page of this book has inveighed against the mistake of allowing industries to do their own regulation, and that particular point need not be made again here. But even when complete safeguards for the public interest have been provided, there is a temptation to leave the management of an industry to the majority vote of those concerned. A characteristic case in point is provided at the time these lines are being written by the negotiations going on between the Government and the cotton industry. The industry has asked the Government to pass through parliament an Enabling Act, which would give the industry legal powers to do certain things, such as fix minimum prices. The Government has, quite rightly, stipulated that certain stringent safeguards for the public shall be written into the scheme. So far so good. But the Government has also stipulated, in effect, that nothing shall be done, either in drawing up the terms of the Enabling Act, or in administering it after its passage into law, except with the approval of a very substantial majority of the industry. Now such a provision may be essential in the circumstances of the case. But its effect will be to condemn the organization thus set up to almost complete impotence. There are very few things indeed that a body of several hundred small competing business men will be able to agree on in principle, once the exploitation both of the consumer and of the public purse is ruled out—and even when they agree in principle, they will disagree in detail. Any such organization means that nothing that is unpopular with more than a tiny proportion of the firms in the industry can be done. But any rationalization of the industry that is worth doing must, almost by definition, be objectionable to many, if not most, of the existing firms.

The absurdity of this system is seen at its clearest in the case of the Milk Marketing Board, whose members are annually elected by more than 200,000 milk producers. The Milk Marketing Scheme has been criticized in Chapter IV.; but apart altogether from the powers and functions which have been so lavishly bestowed upon the Board, it is safe to say that no business enterprise so constituted could succeed. Anybody who tries to run the milk industry as a whole is immediately brought up against the relationship between price and quantity. The more milk there is on the market, the lower will be the average price. But the individual farmer is not in a position to realize the relationship. Price he knows well ; but he cannot see that his score of gallons more or less makes any difference to the price he receives. He is entirely unacquainted with the relationship between price and quantity ; consequently he shouts for higher price coupled with higher production ; and he elects a Board which, for fear of not being re-elected, struggles to find a way out of its dilemma by raising the price to the consumer and dunning the Treasury for subsidies.

The truth is that individual producers cannot be expected to compete with each other (*i.e.* to consider their individual interests) for 364 days a year and on the 365th elect a Board capable of seeing the industry, still less the interests of the community, as a whole. The resulting system is neither individualism nor collectivism, and it is apt to result in the worst of both worlds. It has been called Bastard Socialism, but a better name would be Unsocialism. If the Board elected by the producers is in a position to blackmail the community, it will find that so much the easiest thing to do that it will do nothing else. And if the community wisely protects itself, the producers' Board will accomplish little or nothing. That, at least, has been the experience to date, and looks like being the experience in the future.

When industries are to be organized, let us, then, have no pseudo-democracy of this sort. There may be cases when it is best to leave the existing firms of an industry in possession, but to regulate such matters as prices and productive capacity by some sort of central board. But in these cases the board should be appointed by the state to consist of business men capable of understanding the industry's problems, but independent of it. (It was found during 1914-18 that the best way of controlling an industry was to appoint as controller a capable business man—from another industry.) If it be thought too drastic to give such a board dictatorial powers of compulsion, it might be provided that the industry could reject its findings—but only at the cost of having the whole scheme of reorganization lapse. In other words, the cotton industry, for example, would have the choice of accepting a price-control scheme worked out by an independent board, or of having no price-control scheme at all.

4

Control of this sort, however, is essentially of a negative character. A central controlling authority can frequently impose prohibitions upon individual firms ; it has far fewer weapons of persuading them to take a positive initiative. Many industries in which the state decides to intervene will require considerably more positive central direction.

In cases where an industry has to operate as a unit, it will usually be better for it to be owned as a unit. This was the decision that was very wisely taken when the London Passenger Transport Board was organized. It was recognized that to leave the trams, the buses, the tubes, and the surface railways in separate ownership and separate operation, and to attempt to " co-ordinate " them from some central office was to court failure. Accordingly, the ownership of trams, buses, and tubes was merged in one operating body, and the suburban railways, which could not be divorced from the main lines, were required to pool their receipts with the new combine, which is the next best thing to common ownership.

As an example of the technique of industrial reorganization, the London Passenger Transport Board has two good points and one grave defect. The first good point is that mentioned in the last paragraph—the fact that it is a complete merger, able to operate as a unit and seek the greatest efficiency in so doing. The second good point is that the members of the Board are all chosen not to represent some partial interest, but for their competence to manage the undertaking. Two of them, it is true, are required to have special knowledge of labour and financial matters, but even these two are not nominated by the trade unions and the bankers. The result of these two wise provisions is that the members of the Board are able to devote all their attention to running it in a businesslike way. They are under no temptation either on the one hand to put the interests of buses above trams, or trams above tubes (as they might be if the original owners had been left in existence, and given the right to elect the Board) or to subordinate the interests of the Board's undertaking as a whole to the wishes of its employees or the pockets of its stockholders (as they might if they were elected to " represent " these partial interests).

In these two respects the London Passenger Transport Board can serve as a model for other industrial reorganizations where the state steps in. But in another respect, it stands as a warning. When the London Passenger Transport Board was formed, it purchased the undertakings of its predecessors, paying for them by issuing its own stock. The terms on which the large predecessor undertakings were taken over were, of course, agreed upon by negotiation before the Bill was introduced into parliament. It was only the smaller undertakings whose purchase price had to be fixed by subsequent arbitration, and even then the principles determining the agreements with the larger undertakings were naturally closely followed in the arbitrations. Substantially, then, the price paid by the London Passenger Transport Board, which is the same thing as its capital, was fixed by agreement. This procedure is the natural one to follow in any similar large-scale amalgamation ; no government will be anxious to use strong-arm tactics until it has to, and parliament will always be very susceptible to the cry of injustice or expropriation. But an almost inevitable consequence is that the purchase-price is fixed on the high side, sometimes (not in the case of the London Passenger Transport Board) quite ridiculously on the high side. After all, this is only natural ; the concerns that are being amalgamated are in a position to hold out for good terms, knowing that the Government does not want to have to use compulsion.

The probability is, then, that any large-scale government-sponsored amalgamation starts life with an excessive capitalization. Indeed, over-capitalization is the usual lot of privately-sponsored mergers too. But if a private merger proves to have been over-optimistic in assessing its future earning power, what happens is that the ordinary shareholders, the owners of the equity, get an inadequate dividend. There are disadvantages in that ; but no bones are broken. But the London Passenger Transport Board has no ordinary shareholders. The people who correspond to the equity-owners in the London Passenger Transport Board are the owners of the " C " stock, and though they are not entitled to a fixed dividend every year, they are entitled to a fixed dividend every three years. In 1938 the Board failed, for the third year in succession, to pay this fixed dividend, and, as a result, any group of persons holding more than 5 per cent. of the " C " stock (*i.e.* 1 per cent. of the whole capital of the Board) may apply to the High Court for a receiver to be appointed. The fact that nobody has, at the time these lines are written, actually made application for a receivership does not affect the principle. In principle, every last shilling of the London Passenger

Transport Board's stock is entitled to a fixed rate of interest, with the sanctions of the law available if it is not paid.

Now this is a very dangerous precedent. Compared with many other forms of enterprise, the business of transporting the inhabitants of a great metropolis is a comparatively steady business. But even London Transport cannot reasonably be expected so to manage its affairs that its profits do not vary from year to year. It is a fantastic principle that money can be invested in industry on a wholly fixed-interest basis. And when fixed-interest is combined with over-capitalization, the result is inevitable financial difficulty. If every government-sponsored merger of the future is, first, to be endowed with a generous capitalization, and then to be compelled to pay fixed rates of interest on the whole of it, they will all land in the bankruptcy court—except, perhaps, the few who are in a position to levy sufficient toll on the public and thus defeat the chief aim of their creators. Some degree of over-capitalization is probably unavoidable ; but its evil effects can be reduced to a minimum by providing that as much as possible of the new amalgamated concern's capital shall be of the variable-interest variety.

The origin of the idea that a public board's capital must all be fixed-interest is not economic, but politico-legal. The governing legal principle of joint-stock company organization is that every shareholder must have either the right to a preferential fixed dividend or the right to control the operation of the company by voting for the board of directors. But if a body like the London Passenger Transport Board is being created to serve some grand social purpose, it would be patently absurd to put the control of the board into the hands of a section of the stockholders. *Ergo*, the stockholders, having no voting rights, must have a fixed dividend. It is a very nice legal argument. But it does not make sense. To begin with, we have seen what dangerously rigid financing results from it. And secondly, the legal theory is a legal fiction. There is hardly a large company in existence in which the ordinary shareholders *in fact* (and not merely in law) exercise any control over the management. The four big railway companies, for example, have not been providing very good dividends for their ordinary stockholders in recent years. But do the ordinary stockholders do anything about it? Not one in a thousand ever attends an annual meeting or even sends in a proxy. A company has to be on the very edge of irremediable disaster before the shareholders do anything about it. In general, the position of the equity shareholders in any of our large companies would not be one whit different if they did not possess the theoretical right to elect the directors. If public boards, like the London Passenger Transport Board, issued variable-interest stock, its owners would never know that their position was any different from that of ordinary equity shareholders.

It might, however, be objected that if the directors, or members of a public board, feared neither a receivership petition nor the anger of their stockholders, they would have no incentive to earn reasonable profits. The falsity of this argument might be guessed from the fact, just mentioned, that the directors of the ordinary limited company are normally in no terror of either. And, in fact, the real incentive to profit-earning is different. Any progressive concern has regular need to raise fresh capital, and unless its profits are so enormous as to provide all the money needed (in which case the argument does not arise) they have to persuade investors to part with their money. Before a company can raise money easily its existing stock or shares must be standing at a respectable level on the Stock Exchange. And to do that the directors must pay satisfactory dividends, or at least earn satisfactory profits. The London Passenger Transport Board is in almost constant need of additional capital, and it could raise it far more easily if its " C " stock stood at par or over on the Stock Exchange. This is a more rational incentive to profit-earning than any threats of receivership.

This raises, however, another question. Is profit-earning the only thing for which the administrators of a socialized business are to be given an incentive ? We must not forget that we began this discussion by looking for ways of increasing the efficiency of the economic system in producing goods and services. In general, a socialized industry is betraying its purpose unless it turns out goods and services in greater profusion than it would have done if it had not been socialized. If we create a government-sponsored monopoly, and carefully appoint to manage it independent men who are competent to run it efficiently, and then bother ourselves unduly to provide incentives to profit-earning, are we not in danger of having them act just like private monopolists ? For this reason it is as essential to limit excessive profits as it is to see that reasonable profits are earned. (The limit must not, however, be set too low ; if 5 per cent. is a reasonable *average* return on capital, the limit should be 10 per cent. or thereabouts.) And it might be a good idea to arrange that the personal interests of the managers

should lie with production rather than with profits.
Thus the members of the London Passenger Transport
Board might be given a bonus varying with the number
of passenger-miles run in a year by the Board's vehicles ;
the members of a coal board could be remunerated in
proportion to the number of tons of coal mined, and
so forth. Every competent industrial manager keeps
an eye on both production and profits. But he is only
human if he gives preference to that one of the two
which determines his own income.

But when all is said and done the chief danger in
creating a government-sponsored body to run an industry is that it will be over-conservative, bureaucratic,
slow, stodgy, and unprogressive. The point has already
been made that industries where exceptional alertness
and courage are required should be left to the private
capitalists. But there is no reason why even in those
industries which the state takes over, or in which it decides
to intervene, some of the merits of competition should not
be retained. There is no heaven-sent reason why every
public board has to be a monopoly. In the eager anti-
thesis between free competition and monopoly we have
tended to overlook duopoly. It is probably impracticable
to create a public board for a part only of an industry
(though that has been done). But there is no reason
why, in many industries, there should not be two or three
competing public boards (competing for service, not for
profits) instead of one only.

An example will make clear what is intended. In
Great Britain we have a single monopolist Broadcasting
Corporation, financed by tax revenue and controlled,
ultimately, by the state. In the United States, broadcasting is financed by advertising ; and most of the big

stations are organized in two competing "chains." Having experienced both forms of broadcasting, I am strongly of the opinion that the licence fee and public ownership are better than advertisement-financing. But I am equally strongly of the opinion that the competition between the two chains gives American broadcasting a liveliness and sparkle that contrast very favourably with the British programmes. Would it not be the ideal solution to have two corporations, both financed out of licence fees, but competing for the favour of the listener (who might be allowed to allocate some small fraction of his licence fee—say the final two shillings—to the corporation which pleased him the better) ? If it be objected that this would lead to wasteful duplication of transmitting stations, etc., let these be owned by the state, and hired out to the two corporations on equitable terms.

Another example can be taken from civil aviation. Hitherto there have been two chief British companies operating air services from Great Britain to overseas countries. Of the two, Imperial Airways has been the larger, and has had a semi-official character from the presence of Government directors on its board. But nobody who is acquainted with the two services would deny that the efficiency of Imperial Airways has been increased by the existence of British competition, in the form of British Airways, as well as foreign competition. Towards the end of 1938 proposals were made by the Government for the creation of a publicly owned corporation to take over both Imperial Airways and British Airways. That overseas civil aviation, which has to be heavily subsidized by the Government, should actually be owned by the state is an obviously sensible suggestion. But is there any very good reason why the two competing concerns should not continue to compete in public ownership—and might there not be considerable advantage ? In some other industries, of course, it would be impracticable to have two concerns engaging in direct competition. It would be wasteful, for instance, to have two electricity undertakings supplying the same area. But in these cases healthy rivalry can be provided for by a regional organization. Even if the business of supplying electricity were fully socialized, there would be great virtue in having separate organizations for Lancashire and Yorkshire, so that the two counties might indulge their natural competitive spirit on pence per kilowatt-hour as well as on runs per wicket.

5

This, as promised on page 158, is merely a job lot of suggestions for arranging industrial organization in such a way that efficiency is promoted and not harmed by the entry of the state into the industrial arena. It may be useful to recall very briefly the chief suggestions that have been made.

The plea of Industrial Self-Government has a certain specious appeal to democrats. But it is deceptive. Industrial Self-Government is likely to lead either to exploitation of the public or to futility. Industrial Autocracy is a much more efficient system, provided care is taken to see that the autocrat is responsible to the democratic community.

If every public corporation is endowed with an excessive capitalization on which it has to pay fixed rates of interest, then every extension of public ownership will mean a further subjugation of the economic system to the dead hand of usury. The solution is to finance socialized industries as much as possible by variable-interest stocks, so that the capital-provider, like the labour-provider, may take his share in the ups-and-downs of an unavoidably erratic system.

Those who manage publicly owned industries, apart from being appointed by the state, in its function as trustee for the community, might be remunerated in proportion to the productivity (*i.e.* economic efficiency) of the industries they manage.

Wherever it can be done without wastefulness, public corporations should compete with one another, and for this reason the aim should be to create two or more corporations in each industry instead of one.

It is, however, perhaps advisable to repeat, as a last word, what was said before on page 153. These suggestions should be found helpful in maintaining efficiency in those cases in which the state decides to intervene. But the length at which they have been discussed must not be taken as meaning that state intervention is a universally applicable prescription. On the contrary, there are cases in which it is right, and others in which it is wrong. And that state of affairs will last for as long as any man now living can foresee.

CHAPTER IX

THE PURSUIT OF EQUALITY

I

IF the need for a very much greater degree of economic equality has not received, in the last few chapters, as much emphasis as it might be thought to deserve, the omission has not in any way been due to any lack of appreciation of its urgency, but rather because it is both obvious and familiar. Of recent years, the passion for greater equality of incomes and welfare has become, for many people, the mainspring of all thinking on economic problems. There are dangers in this—certainly if equality is pursued regardless of its effects on the size and regularity of the income that is to be shared. But it is an understandable and generous emotion ; above all, it is a democratic emotion. The perfect democracy would not need to insist on an absolute equality of economic welfare among its citizens ; but it could hardly operate so long as there were such enormous differences in political power, economic welfare, and personal privilege as exist in our present society. Such differences as were allowed to exist should clearly be related, however imperfectly, to personal merits or achievements. A democracy is not a democracy if some persons, by mere accident of birth, belong to an order of creation noticeably superior to the majority of their fellow men. Just as political democracy is incompatible with a hereditary ruling caste, so economic democracy cannot be reconciled with a hereditary plutocracy. Absolute equality of income need not be insisted on ; but complete equality of opportunity is an essential element of democracy—and that will not be possible without a very great reduction in the present inequality of incomes.

The reduction of inequality must, therefore, be considered to be one of the essential objects of any democratic economic policy—as an immediate object, what is more, not as one to be deferred until other objects have been secured. It cannot wait.

It does not in the least diminish the sincerity of this statement to add that the pursuit of equality must be undertaken with caution. To take away the wealth of the rich and hand it over to the poor is comparatively easy ; organized highway robbery would do, or the repeal of all laws protecting property. But we can all agree that this method of seeking equality would be worse than the inequality it would be aimed at. We must constantly ask what will follow the redistribution of wealth. If the methods chosen are such that the productive mechanism is disrupted, it may turn out to be poverty rather than wealth that is equally shared. In the terminology that has been used throughout this book, any increase in Equality which substantially reduced the Efficiency or the Adaptability of the economic system would be damaging to the community. In more concrete terms, a reduction in the inequality of incomes which also brought about a reduction in the total national income would be retrogression rather than progress.

There are some people who would question this last statement. So passionate is their hatred of inequality that they would sacrifice *some* of the community's income to secure a more equal distribution of what remained. Now, in pure theory, we may all agree that it would be worth sacrificing a *very little* of the communal income for a *very great* gain in Equality ; just as, incidentally, it would be worth sacrificing a *very little* Equality for a *very great* gain in income. But the trouble about all such statements is that, first, nobody can ever agree on what constitutes a small sacrifice or a large gain ; and, secondly, that since nobody can be sure in advance of exactly what is going to be the effect of a given economic measure (save that it is likely to be less favourable than its sponsors estimate), to set out with the object of reducing income very slightly is probably to finish up by reducing it very considerably. There is so much poverty in the world to-day that no risks should be run with the Efficiency of the economic mechanism. It is a safe rule to follow that no steps should be taken to reduce inequality that would be likely actually to reduce the communal income. The utmost concession that can be made is that it may be permissible, for a very large increase in Equality, to risk a slowing down of the pace at which the communal income increases. And even that is playing with fire. Any such proposals, in any case, are the less necessary because it is fully possible (I am convinced) to advance Equality without hindering Efficiency or Adaptability. That is the only way of being quite sure that the process of levelling is one of levelling up, not of levelling down.

2

Economic inequality has two facets, each of them equally obnoxious. In the first place there is the poverty of the poor—not the unavoidable poverty due to the fact that the income of the community as a whole is limited, but the avoidable poverty due to the fact that such wealth as exists is so unequally distributed. For example, if the community as a whole is not wealthy enough to have a motor car for every family (*i.e.* if it would rather devote its limited resources to something else), then we cannot fairly blame on the inequality of incomes the fact that millions of poor families do not have a car. But if thousands of under-nourished children in need of milk live in a country where milk is sold at less than cost of production for making into products of less nutritive value than fresh milk, such a scandalous state of affairs can fairly be laid at the door of inequality. The community manifestly can afford the milk necessary to provide the minimum for every child—it produces most of it already—and the fact that the milk is not used where it would do most good is the result of the inequality of incomes.

The other aspect of the inequality of incomes which is harmful is the wealth of the wealthy. If we can draw a " poverty line " and say that anybody below it has too little, then equally we can draw an " affluence line " and say that anybody above it has too much. Money always breeds corruption, and there are half a hundred subtle ways in which the political and economic scales are tilted in favour of the very rich. Apart from this, the existence of great wealth and the social emulation to which it gives rise result in a great deal of sheer economic waste. The sight of great wealth is as disgusting as the sight of poverty is distressing.

The task of reducing inequality is thus one of lopping off both extremities. To a large extent the two problems are the same. But it is nevertheless practically useful to draw a distinction between them—if only for the reason that the prevention of poverty is an aim that will collect much more popular support than the prevention of excessive wealth. Let us, therefore, leave for the moment the more controversial end of the problem of inequality and see what can be done in the immediate future to prevent the excesses of poverty.

The chief weapon for advancing this policy is that familiar under the title of the National Minimum. The basic idea of the National Minimum is that a minimum standard of elementary necessities should be laid down and that every citizen should be guaranteed that minimum as of right. The state has never deliberately adopted the policy of the National Minimum as such. But in practice, it has taken a number of steps in that direction. For example, every child is now guaranteed a free education until the age of 14 to 15 years. The scale of allowances drawn up by the Unemployment Assistance Board is, in effect, a minimum scale of income below which no unemployed family should fall. In many badly-paid industries, the state has set up Trade Boards to enforce a scale of minimum wages. In housing, the slum-clearance programme sets a standard of dilapidation (open to considerable variation in interpretation) below which dwellings must not fall, while the overcrowding legislation defines the minimum space that every human being must have.

But though much has been done, much remains to be done. To begin with, there are many gaps in our national set of minima. One gap which has been receiving increasing attention in the last few years is that of food. The scientists have succeeded in drawing up scales of properly balanced diets for men, women, and children. According to one investigation, the diets of half the population could be increased with benefit to their health, while a substantial portion are definitely under-nourished. We need to set a national minimum standard of nutrition, and see that every family has the means to attain it. There are similar gaps on the side of health. The National Health Insurance scheme has done wonders in improving the health of the workers of the country. But it leaves their wives and families unprovided for. And there are many services (*e.g.* infant welfare centres) which are only available in some districts (1939).

Secondly, even when the gaps in the existing standard have been closed, there is still room for very great improvement in the standard itself. Some of our minima are very inadequate. This is true, for example, of housing, where the definitions both of what constitutes a slum and of what constitutes overcrowding are very far below what the ordinary man and woman would understand by the same terms. Among the health services, eyes and teeth are largely neglected (the state of British teeth, in particular, is very bad). We are definitely behind other countries in the provision of secondary education. Many other progressive countries provide completely free secondary education, without any test of scholarship, even if they do not compel attendance. In the United States, though the legal definition of leaving age varies from state to state, " school age " is defined as from 5 to 17 years, and nearly 85 per cent. of the children of school age are actually enrolled in the schools ; an amendment to the Constitution has been passed by Congress (though not yet ratified by the states) permitting the entire prohibition of the labour of persons under eighteen years of age.

The completion and improvement of the National Minimum must therefore be the first task of a policy of increasing Equality. I would suggest that two scales be drawn up—the Irreducible Minimum and the Decent Minimum. The difference between them may be illustrated by an example ; it is possible to draw up a minimum dietary just sufficient for adequate nutrition which includes no fresh milk, but only condensed skimmed milk in tins (*e.g.* Mr. Seebohm Rowntree's diet in *The Human Needs of Labour*) ; but any " decent minimum " ought to include fresh unskimmed milk at least for children. Each " minimum " should cover food, clothing, houseroom, heating, education, and medical care. The aim should be to establish the Irreducible Minimum at the earliest possible moment—as a matter of urgency—and to reach the Decent Minimum by a defined series of precise stages over the shortest possible number of years.

The minimum once established, every citizen should be entitled to it as of right, without any taint of Poor Law or charity. The exact way of providing the different items will naturally vary from case to case. For education, it is obviously more economical and more effective to provide the schools free and compel attendance at them. For medical services, the combination of insurance for some services and free hospitals or clinics for others is established and works tolerably well. In the case of houses, the method is to give subsidies out of public funds to lower the rents charged and, very broadly speaking, this is also a satisfactory method. But for all the requirements which cannot be specifically made available in this way, the only method of ensuring the attainment of the National Minimum is to assess the cost, varying from time to time and from place to place, of providing it and to see that every individual has sufficient income for the purpose. There will always be some fathers who will drink the money for the children's shoes. But if once it were established that every family had money enough to buy shoes, the failure to provide them could be made evidence of neglect and punishable by law. It should be an offence to under-feed children just as it is now an offence to overcrowd them.

Mention of children leads to the centre of the problem of poverty. Every social worker and slum parson knows that poverty is largely a matter of children. The slums and the overcrowded houses are inhabited by children. The Overcrowding Survey of 1935 divided the families of the country into two groups—those that were, and those that were not, overcrowded (on the official definition of the term). As was only reasonable to expect, the overcrowded families were, on the average, larger than the non-overcrowded families. But what the Survey also observed was that the overcrowded family, although it was 80 per cent. larger than the non-overcrowded family, occupied a dwelling that was, on the average, actually 38 per cent. *smaller*. The overcrowding of large families is not due merely to the fact that they are large, but also to the fact that they cannot afford even as roomy a dwelling as the smaller family. Surveys of nutrition lead to very much the same result : the more children there are in a family, the lower is the average standard of nutrition. The story is the same in education ; where the family is large, the children are compelled to leave school and find work on the earliest permissible day, however promising they may be. It is not enough merely to provide " free places " at secondary schools for promising children ; it may not be enough to provide grants to pay for their keep. The child who works can make a net contribution to the family's exchequer, and where there is severe poverty, that net contribution is the decisive factor.

This inequality of incomes between families is the chief direct cause of extreme poverty in this country to-day. In every trade and industry, it is broadly true to say that the minimum wages paid to-day are enough to keep the small family above the poverty line. It is the large family that breeds poverty—and that is the same thing as saying that there is a much higher proportion of the nation's *children* than of the nation's inhabitants as a whole below the poverty line. Strangely enough, this particular aspect of inequality has never received nearly as much attention as it deserves, especially from those professional denouncers of inequality, the leaders of organized labour. But it must receive urgent attention if poverty and inequality are to be removed. Perhaps one reason why the trade unions keep quiet about this matter is that it shows the impossibility—or at least the immense difficulty—of solving the problem of poverty by increasing the standard rate of wages. It is clearly useless to tackle the problem by assuming that all families are of equal size. It is no good passing legislation that provides a decent house for the *average* family, since the larger-than-average family will still be overcrowded. (It is no good, incidentally, laying down a standard of overcrowding and punishing those who transgress it, unless the over-large family is at the same time helped to afford a larger house. If it is not given such help, the net result will be to compel it to spend more on rent and less on food.) It is equally no good passing legislation to enforce the payment of a minimum wage sufficient to support the *average* family. The National Minimum must be calculated, not on a *family* basis, but on an *individual* basis. And if it is objected that the parents of large families will then be taking out of the national pool more than they put in, the fair answer can be made that they are providing the community with the one element indispensable to its continuance—progeny.

3

We must return now to the more controversial end of the problem of inequality. The policy of the National Minimum would remove excessive poverty. How are we to prevent excessive wealth?

Much the greater part of the excessively large incomes comes from the ownership of property. It arises in the form of rent, interest, and profits. The simplest and most direct way of getting rid of excessive incomes would therefore seem to be to reduce the amounts paid out in rent, interest, and profits. But after all that has been said in previous chapters, it is hardly necessary to argue here that this particular method would do more harm to Efficiency than it would do good to Equality. If I say that our economy must be a capitalist one, I am running the risk of being misunderstood, since the word " capitalist " has acquired in popular usage a peculiar meaning. But what is true is that our economy depends for its smooth and efficient working on the investment of capital. It does so in two ways ; it is necessary to have a high and increasing volume of capital equipment if the productive efficiency of the system is to be large enough to abolish poverty ; and it is necessary to have a regular and uninterrupted investment of capital if we are to avoid periodical relapses into unemployment. Now interest and profits [1] are the income and reward of capital. So long as any capital is left in private ownership, the net effect of reducing interest and profits (by special taxation or by unduly increasing labour costs) will be to reduce the investment of capital. It will hurt the community, including the poor. It is not a method of promoting Equality that we can approve.

If interest and profit cannot be abolished so long as capital remains in private hands, many people draw the logical conclusion that capital must be taken out of private ownership. This is the origin of the Socialist demand for the "nationalization of all the means of production, distribution, and exchange." It was argued in the last chapter that, on the score of improving Efficiency, nationalization may in some cases be a necessary device—just as it is likely to be wasteful in other cases. In any event, there is no reason to have any prejudice against public ownership as a means of promoting Efficiency.

But as a means of promoting Equality, nationalization of industry is likely to be, at best, very slow and ineffective. There are three main reasons for this. One is that there are many industries in which public ownership

---

[1] Rent is a peculiar case, having some of the characteristics of interest and some of its own. There is, unfortunately, no room to discuss this complicated matter here.

would be so damaging to productive Efficiency that it must be ruled out on that account. No sensible man can foresee a state of affairs—at least a democratic state of affairs—in which there will not be large sectors of the national economy under private control and in private ownership. Secondly, even in the field that is proper to it, the extension of public ownership, if it is not to create damaging disturbance, will necessarily be very gradual. The third reason is the most important. No democratic body of Socialists advocates the confiscation of privately owned capital ; they all advocate the payment of reasonable compensation. Indeed, confiscation could not be carried through in a democratic country where there are millions of people owning some form of property. But if fair compensation is to be paid, there is no reduction in the amount, but only in the form, of property held by private persons. The individuals who formerly owned the nationalized industry will draw interest instead of profits. True, there might be small savings if nationalized industries were given the guarantee of the state for their capital and were therefore able to borrow it at the low gilt-edged rate. But the general grant of state guarantees would be a very questionable policy ; the amounts thus saved would be very small ; and there is good reason for believing that, in many cases, public administration might be just sufficiently less efficient than private administration to cancel out this saving.

It is possible that a thoroughgoing policy of nationalization, pushed as far and as fast as it could be without damaging Efficiency, might contribute a little to the reduction of inequality. But, for my part, I consider the question of Equality too urgent to wait for this tortoise-like solution.

As was pointed out in Chapter II., the real root of the inequality of incomes is not so much the private ownership of property as the inheritance of property. If inheritance were abolished, we could safely leave all the other factors—profits, interest, high salaries for rare brands of skill, etc.—unchanged and nevertheless reduce the volume of inequality to an amount that we could afford to ignore.

Since inheritance is the root of the trouble, the best way is to attack it directly. Some would carry the logic so far as to advocate the total abolition of the inheritance of property. There is something to be said, in a purely philosophical sense, for such a drastic remedy. But for practical purposes we can dismiss it entirely from consideration. There is no prospect whatever of such a measure being democratically adopted. And in any case we ought to be chary of limiting the sums that a man can bequeath to his children, or even to his grandchildren, since the desire to do so is one of the most powerful stimuli to individual effort and exertion, upon which, in the last resort, the whole wealth of the community is based.

But though the abolition of inheritance is neither a practicable nor a prudent proposal, the state has for many decades imposed taxation on the inheritance of property. These death duties are so heavy, and are claimed by those who have to pay them to be so crippling, that they might be thought to be effecting already a considerable transfer of wealth. Now it is beyond doubt true that some family fortunes have been very considerably diminished by death duties. A family which is unfortunate enough to have two generations die in rapid succession can be very badly hit. But in general and on the average, as has already been remarked on page 37, there is very little sign that the death duties are noticeably reducing the inequality of wealth. The high rates of duty have now been in force for two decades, and in that period the majority of the property of the country must have passed by inheritance. But there are more people with incomes of over £8,000 nowadays than there were people with incomes of over £5,000 before 1914, and the number of millionaires dying seems to increase year by year.

If the inequality of incomes is to be diminished by taxation on inheritance, then the rates of duty will have to be very considerably increased. To many people this will appear an alarming statement. Indeed, if the rates of taxation in 1939 were simply doubled, they would be entirely confiscatory at the highest levels, and harmful consequences might well follow. But a method of collecting death duties has been suggested which, I believe, overcomes these difficulties. A man's desire to leave property to his children is strong, to his grand-children less strong. Very few men, when they are making efforts and sacrifices to accumulate a fortune, think of the welfare of their great-grandchildren, and none at all of their great-great-grandchildren. Yet there are thousands of people living in affluence to-day because of the wealth made by their great-grandfathers or even remoter ancestors. If it could be provided that a man could leave the greater part of his fortune to his children, and that a substantial portion of it should be passed on to his grandchildren, but very little to his great-grand-children, and none at all to his great-great-grandchildren, a large part of the evil of inherited inequality would be swept away without diminishing the incentive to men of energy and enterprise to make as much money as they can. The proposal is that when a man, A, dies and leaves his property to his son, B, in addition to death duties levied as at present, a further sum, perhaps equal to the first, should be paid to the state, but not until B's death. An alternative version is that on A's death, two death duties should be charged, but that the second portion should bear interest during the lifetime of B.

We are here concerned not with the exact version, but with the main principle, and the only other technical point that should be mentioned is that if the rates of death duty are going to be materially increased, the state will have to accept payment in means other than cash. As it is, when death duties of a third or so of the value of an estate have to be paid in cash, the heirs have great difficulty in disposing of enough property to raise the sums required.

But I do not think the state need be very frightened of accepting payment in kind. There is at least one large insurance company in England whose managers administer property, of all sorts and varieties, of a value of over £300,000,000, and there seems to be no good reason why the state should not also form similar trusts to administer, in complete independence, property belonging to it. If death duties of the present amount continued to be paid in cash, while a second instalment of equal value is handed over in kind, interest on which was to be paid for one generation, the amount of property coming in these " second instalments " would be of the order of £80,000,000 a year. If the state formed a new trust every five years or so, to administer this property on the advice of a group of skilled investment experts, and to pay out the income, *pro rata*, to the beneficiaries or (after their death) to the state, it would be attempting a no more difficult task than is at present accomplished by the directors and managers of the Prudential Assurance Company Limited. As the beneficiaries died off and income began to accrue to the state, it could be used either to reduce taxation or to extend the National Minimum. In any case, to avoid the accusation that death duties result in the consumption of capital for current needs, the trusts should be kept intact. In this way the state would gradually acquire title to what may be called the excess property of the very rich. Since it is only on the very rich that the rates of death duties are very heavy, this plan would not lead to the concentration in the hands of the state of all the community's property, but merely of that part of it that is above the " affluence line."

I believe that some such plan as this, if it were carefully thought out and prudently administered, would be the means of achieving a substantial reduction in the present inequality of wealth, without (and here it differs vitally from other schemes for reducing inequality) having any harmful effects either on Efficiency or on Regularity. As for Efficiency, the effect would be harmful only if it can be supposed that men would work less hard if they knew that their great-grandchildren would derive no benefit from their present efforts—a supposition which seems wholly unreasonable. As for Regularity, the existence in public control of large funds of more or less liquid capital might be used to produce that greater regularity of the investment of money in capital equipment which is one of the main desiderata for avoiding business fluctuations.

Lest it be thought that the proposal of a system of death duties progressive over time (usually known, from its inventor, as the Rignano scheme) is either Utopian or inequitable, it may be mentioned that the Colwyn Committee, a very strong body of practical financiers and economists, examined the proposal several years ago. They did not recommend its adoption ; but they found that it was " not impracticable," although great care would have to be taken to ensure fairness between individuals, and they stated that " some of us find the principle in itself attractive, and think it possible . . . that it may in course of time have useful developments and enable some improvement to be effected in the existing death duties system." In view of the conservative opinions of the signatories of this report [they were Lord Colwyn, Sir Charles Addis, Sir Alan Anderson (later M.P. for the City of London), Sir Arthur Balfour (now Lord Riverdale), Mr. Henry Bell, Mr. W. L. Hichens, Sir William McLintock, and Lord (then Sir Josiah) Stamp], this quotation is sufficient warrant, especially after the experience of the many intervening years, for advocating some such scheme as the major item in a programme for reducing the inequality of wealth.

4

Apart from this major item, two other matters seem to be worthy of mention. We suffer not only from inequality of inherited wealth, but also from inequality of economic privilege, which is not quite the same thing. Everybody in Great Britain knows how important it is, in getting one of the best jobs, to have been to the right school or the right university. This sort of unequal privilege helps many men, even without a penny of inherited wealth, to get jobs better than they are really worth. By the same token it prevents men who have not had the " correct " education from getting the jobs they do deserve. This is not only wrong in itself ; it results in economic waste, since it prevents the best use being made of the human material available.

This tyranny of the " correct " education is far stronger than those who benefit from it are prepared to admit. But it is an incontrovertible fact that the boys who have been to the right sort of school form a much higher proportion of the undergraduates in our universities, and especially at Oxford and Cambridge, than can be justified by any considerations of their proportion of the total population or of their relative intelligence. Nor is this quite the same thing as saying that the rich can give their sons better education than the poor. The usefulness, in cash terms, of the " correct " education is such that thousands of middle-class families who cannot afford it stint themselves in order to send their sons to " correct " schools. It is not that they think the educa-tion at the " correct " schools is any better than at the state schools ; it is not entirely due to snobbery, for many of these parents are confirmed believers in social equality. It is simply recognition of the hard fact that a boy who has been to one of these schools has a very much better chance of earning a good living than if he had spent just as many years applying himself with the same intelligence to the same subjects but in a different school.

This peculiar form of inequality of privilege, which exists in no other country, is the source of a very great deal of economic waste in Great Britain. But it is very difficult to know what to do about it, especially since many of those who dislike it most feel unable to disregard it, lest they should be penalizing their children. The least that can be done is for the state to stop its disguised support of the system (*e.g.* by formerly permitting " Officers' Training Corps " at the " Public Schools," but only cadet corps at other schools). The state might go a long way to compel these select schools to offer a large number of " free places " to deserving children from the public elementary schools ; the state could use the weapon of refusing recognition as efficient schools to those institutions that refused to comply. Another measure that would help would be to improve the status and pay of the teacher in the state schools. Perhaps the most effective means would be a vast increase in the number of public secondary schools, and in the proportion of all children going to them. If the school leaving age were raised to 17 to 18 years, and entry to the universities were made genuinely competitive, the peculiar privilege of the " Old School Tie " would soon be drowned out. Until it is, there can be no genuine equality.

Another similar matter in which Equality and Efficiency march hand in hand is in the necessity for reform in the methods by which business chiefs are selected. The curse of British business is nepotism. The principle that those who own the capital of a business should appoint its managers is so deep-rooted that it cannot be upset, and where, as in a family business, one man or a small group of men do genuinely and entirely own a business, it is only right and proper that they should manage it. But what is distasteful, inequitable, and uneconomic is the method by which business leaders are selected in public companies, where the directors frequently own only a fraction of the capital invested. In many businesses there is a rigid line drawn between " principals," who are a race capable of becoming directors, and " employees," who are kept where they belong. Nobody who knows, for example, the City of London and Wall Street can fail to be impressed by the fact that in Wall Street there is a continuous ladder open to the able and ambitious man leading from the junior clerkship to the senior partnership, whereas in London the able man progresses more in spite of than with the aid of his employers. A similar comparison between the industrial personnel of Great Britain, on the one hand, and of either Russia or the United States on the other, would lead to similar conclusions. It is not untrue to say that those British businesses in which any particular trouble is taken to see that the most capable and efficient man gets the most important job are in a minority. This, again, is a matter that is easy to criticize, but difficult to remedy. The rule should be made that in all public enterprises, appointments should be made by some method that ensures that merit is the only consideration—say by examination for lower posts, and by committee selection for the higher posts. And for all public companies it might be a salutary rule if the name and salary of every employee related by blood or marriage to any member of the Board of Directors had to be published.

If the business of a country is inefficiently managed, the community as a whole suffers. It is, therefore, in the community's paramount interest to take what steps it can to promote the efficiency of management even in businesses which are technically private. It must never be forgotten that every company which enjoys the benefits of being incorporated with limited liability has received a privilege from the state which might, in times of difficulty, be of enormous value to it. No such company is in a strong moral position to deny the truth of the principle enunciated by Franklin D. Roosevelt, that " private office is a public trust." Already the law provides that a company director (whose legal position is akin to that of a trustee) has obligations of honesty above those imposed on the ordinary citizen. It is only a step further to recognize that the state, as well as the shareholders, has an interest in his efficiency as well as his honesty.

In a great many of the matters that have been discussed in this book, we have discovered that a democratic economy requires the application to economic matters of principles identical with, or similar to, those first applied to political matters by the French Revolution. This is particularly true here ; for all that we are urging is that in business as in politics the principle by which men are selected for responsibility and power should genuinely be *la carrière ouverte aux talents*. Only so shall we secure both Efficiency and Equality.

CHAPTER X

REGULARITY

I

WHENEVER, in the course of this book, we have turned our attention to the third of our trinity of economic objectives we have had to emphasize its differences from the other two. The demand for Regularity is a comparative new-comer; it is only within the lifetime of most of us that it has been elevated to the dignity of a major aim of economic policy. One hundred and fifty years ago it was accepted as axiomatic that the sole aim of economic policy was to increase the productivity—what we have called the Efficiency—of the economic system, in order to reduce poverty. Fifty years ago, most thinking people had come to admit that a greater degree of economic equality should be set alongside the pursuit of Efficiency as an object of policy. But at neither period was the irregularity of the economic system, and its chief manifestation, unemployment, regarded as more than an incidental by-product of the workings of the machine. It is only in our own day that the removal of unemployment has been made the chief economic task of governments. It would have been inconceivable to earlier generations that governments, in attempting to remove unemployment, should, as often now happens,

REGULARITY

deliberately restrict the productivity, or increase the inequality of the economic machine.

The pursuit of Regularity, moreover, differs in a more
important sense from its two companions. The Efficiency of the economic system, if left to itself, slowly
increases. The task of conscious policy, so far as
Efficiency is concerned, is to speed up an existing natural
process, and to see that it is not impeded. Similarly
with Equality, the aim is mainly to speed up a process
that is already partially in existence, and to make up
our minds whether we are prepared to face the drastic
measures that will be necessary if we are to make satisfactory progress towards Equality. But in the case of
Regularity, the evil seems to be getting worse rather
than better. Indeed, there are reasons—to be reviewed
in a minute—for believing that, left to itself, the economic
system will get more and more irregular in the production of wealth, even though the *average* volume of its
production may steadily rise, and the distribution of it
among the individuals who compose the community
may get steadily more equitable.

Further, it is easy to lay down in theoretical terms what
is necessary to cure poverty and inequality, even though
the practical application of the remedies may be very
difficult. But when it comes to the system's irregularity,
no such confident diagnosis is possible. In the last three
chapters, which dealt with poverty and inequality, a
main remedy for each defect was found. For poverty,
the remedy is a plentiful application of capital. For
inequality, the remedy is a limitation, or gradual abolition, of the inheritance of property. But for irregularity, the prescription has no main constituent, and the
cure cannot be expected to be perfect.

The last task to be tackled in this book is therefore the most difficult. But the path will be smoothed to some extent if we first carefully state the nature of the periodic fits of indigestion that afflict the economic system. It was pointed out in Chapter II. that every explanation of the trade cycle that has been competently put forward defines it as some form of *maladjustment*. We can go further. Fluctuations of trade are due to a maladjustment between, on the one hand, the amount and variety of the goods and services demanded and, on the other hand, the amount and variety of the goods that the community is equipped to supply. The various theorists of the trade cycle differ and quarrel about what causes these maladjustments between demand and supply to arise, and about what cures should be attempted. But they would all, I think, agree upon the definition here stated.

A depression arrives when the individuals composing the community become, for some reason, unwilling or unable to buy goods and services in the exact quantities and varieties that these same individuals, in their capacity as producers, are able and willing to supply. The opposite state of affairs, a boom, occurs when the individuals composing the community start falling over each other in their eagerness to buy more goods and services than they themselves can produce. It will help us all through this chapter if we keep before our eyes the picture of economic irregularity being due to a tendency for the community's demand—not merely for some specific sorts of goods, but for goods and services in general—sometimes to exceed the community's capacity to supply and sometimes to fall below it. And since slumps are much more unpleasant than booms, we can concern ourselves most with the tendency of demand **to** be periodically insufficient.

2

Why is the irregularity of the system getting worse? It is possible to distinguish four main reasons, or sets of reasons.

The first arises directly out of the fact that we are now at a comparatively high standard of development. It has been argued in earlier chapters that the world does not yet produce enough to satisfy its minimum reasonable needs. Even a rich economic organism like Great Britain finds it impossible to guarantee the Decent Minimum. But while this is perfectly true, it is also true that we approach more closely, in our day and age, to sufficiency than ever before. We have much more to consume than our grandfathers or even our fathers did. But obviously the more we have, the more we can at a pinch do without. When the total consumption of the mass of men is no more than the absolute minimum necessary to keep them alive from day to day, consumption (*i.e.* demand) cannot be reduced. If the minimum is all that the community can supply, then demand cannot fall below supply. But the higher our normal demand gets above the absolute short-period minimum, the more we can reduce our actual demand if the adversity of a slump compels us to. There is, consequently, an inherent tendency for the richer nations to have the deeper depressions.

This tendency works also in a different way. The greater the element of luxury in the normal consumption of a community the more fickle it is, not only in total quantity but in variety. There is little possibility of changeability in the subsistence minimum. Bread is bread and shoddy is shoddy. But when we get into the luxury class, especially those sections where fashion rules, change is of the essence of demand. Supply, however, cannot change with the same rapidity as demand. When the ladies cease to wear plumes in their hats and spend their money on silk stockings instead, the plumage birds cannot be instantaneously converted into silkworms, nor can the men who lead expeditions in search of rare birds settle down at once to breed mulberry trees on the hill-sides of Japan. Those who trim the plumes do not immediately find work in the hosiery mills. In short, every time the nature of demand alters, some section of the population loses its livelihood, is compelled to restrict its own consumption, and breeds a slump-germ. When the changes in taste are world-wide and important (*e.g.* the preference for water-power and oil-power over coal, or for newer fabrics over cotton, or for other foodstuffs over wheat) the effects are often serious.

A particular and very important variety of the instability of demand in a highly developed society is the instability of demand for capital goods. It is capital, as we have seen, that enables man to produce more and more as time goes on. The more highly developed an economic system is, the more of its output of goods and services is assisted by capital and the greater the proportion of its income it devotes to producing new capital. Now capital goods, almost by definition, are goods whose usefulness extends over a considerable period of time. They are not consumed by a single use—and that is equivalent to saying that they do not necessarily have to be produced at virtually the same time as they are consumed. It follows that even if capital goods are *used* fairly regularly, they can be *produced* in fits and starts. And that, in point of fact, is what tends to happen. For reasons that it is far beyond the scope of this book to attempt to explain, the community tends to produce a decade's supply of capital goods in three or four years. That means, of course, that a supply of labour and capital has to be maintained in the industries which produce capital goods far larger than would be necessary if the production were more regularly spread. And during the other years this equipment and labour stand idle, forced to pull in their belts and go on the dole. In short, in these idle years the community is not demanding the goods it is equipped to supply, partly because it is equipped to supply, in a year, more capital goods than it requires in an average year, and partly because, in the lean years, it does not order even its average requirement of capital goods. Clearly, the more advanced a community is, the more seriously will it be affected by this alternating over-employment and under-employment of the capital goods industries.

This is the first set of reasons why irregularity is tending to get worse. The second set arises out of the greatly increased efforts that have been made in the last two generations consciously to shape and control the economic organism. This is a paradoxical state of affairs. For the greatest impelling force behind the state's interventions in business is the desire to prevent unemployment. It is the threat of unemployment that leads industries to clamour for protective duties, or compulsory price-fixing powers, or subsidies of one sort or another. Nevertheless, these policies frequently have the indirect effect of creating more unemployment than they remove. True, they usually achieve their immediate purpose in the industries to which they are directly applied. The protective duty on steel imports increases the volume of employment in the British steel industry. But it also enables the steel industry to raise its prices above the world level. This creates unemployment in two ways. In the first place, the competitive ability of all steel-using export trades is adversely affected. And secondly, everything containing steel that is sold on the home market increases in price, so that the purchasing power of the home population is restricted.

This argument must not, of course, be pressed too far. Not every sort of intervention by the state has this result. But it is unfortunately true that many of them do. Politicians are beings who take action much more easily under strong pressure from injured interests than in accordance with logical and consistent principles. It is inevitable that a large number of the state's economic interventions should be at the behest of industries that are suffering from progress. But every time that a natural progressive shift in demand is prevented from having its normal painful effect on the mechanism of supply, every time an industry that should be shrinking is encouraged by the state to resist the pressure, another pool of unused or incompletely used resources of capital and labour is created.

Since we neither wish to prevent changes in demand, nor are able to do so even if we wished to, the interests of the community are best served if the process of adaptation is assisted as much as possible, not impeded. The pangs of child-birth are admittedly excruciatingly painful to the mother. But the proper way to deal with them is by preventing them from being felt, not by impeding the processes that cause them. Similarly, the task of easing the discomforts of economic rebirth is to find means of anæsthetising the sufferer without impeding the changes. Too many of our economic devices (*i.e.* the mass of coal legislation passed since the Twenties) attempt to prevent the painful contraction, and to keep as many mines and men as possible in a state of semi-employment, at considerable cost to the community, rather than permit change to occur. And as the practice of state intervention increases, more and more of such impediments to organic change can be expected. Their net effect will be to increase the irregularity of the economic system.

A third cause of growing irregularity is to be found in the working of modern monetary systems. Economic actions take effect through the instrumentality of money. What is really a process of bartering goods and services for goods and services is transmuted into buying and selling for money. The ideal monetary system would be one which faithfully carried out the economic intentions of the public without distorting the impulses on the way. Unfortunately, such a monetary system has yet to be discovered. There is no convincing reason to suppose that the ideal monetary system would be reached when the quantity of money in existence remained absolutely fixed, or if it fluctuated in proportion to the population, or in proportion to the volume of industrial production. But it is true that a monetary system in which the volume of money fluctuates violently, especially if its fluctuations are purely arbitrary, is almost certainly a bad one, which adds instabilities of its own to those that arise from the underlying economic conditions of supply and demand.

Unfortunately credit, which is more and more taking the place of hard cash, is from its nature an elusive element, and we know from experience that it is highly volatile. The growth of credit is another reason for expecting a gradual increase in the irregularity of the economic system. Some day we may be able to cancel this conclusion, when the money-managers have succeeded in bringing money under conscious and successful control. Up to the present, however, it has to be sorrowfully admitted that the management of money has more often increased than diminished the disturbing effect of industrial fluctuations.

The final reason for expecting a gradual increase in irregularity is to be found in the fact that the total size of the community—its population—is ceasing to increase and will soon begin to decline. The economic effects of a stationary or a declining population have hardly yet been worked out, but it is almost certain that a greater degree of economic " indigestion " will be one of them. Economic indigestion, or unemployment, comes about when a stagnant pool of idle resources of labour and capital is left without demand for the products it is equipped and ready to produce. The disappearance of demand may be permanent or temporary—permanent if the demand for the products of a particular industry has been reduced by lasting technological or political changes (e.g. the British coal or cotton industries) ; temporary if it is due to the periodic postponement of the purchase of capital goods.

Both varieties are made more likely by stagnating population. In the first place, when the population is rapidly increasing, many a " declining " industry merely fails to share in the general advance. It can contract in relative size merely by standing still. The resources of labour and capital located in the industry when it begins to contract are not rendered unremunerative ; they merely fail to increase and gradually disappear as they retire from activity. But in a stationary community no such comfortable fading-away is possible. If people decide to spend a smaller fraction of their incomes on the products of a certain industry, that industry is faced with immediate painful shrinkage. Secondly, an expanding society has a much smaller possibility than a stationary one of postponing its orders for capital goods. Population in such a community does not stop increasing when a slump comes, and before long a supply of houses, baking machinery, and transport for the increasing numbers is urgently needed. A stationary society's ability to postpone orders for capital goods, on the other hand, is limited only by the slow wearing-out of the existing stock of such goods. Others things being equal, a community whose population is not increasing will tend to suffer from more violent fluctuations in its national income than one that is rapidly expanding—although the movement of its *average* national income, taken over good years and bad, will, of course, be much smaller.

For these four sets of reasons, there would seem to be a tendency for the trade cycle to get worse. Even in combination, however, they are no more than a tendency— a tendency that could be combated if we set ourselves consciously to do so.

3

What, then, can be done to prevent the economic system from getting into this periodic state of maladjustment between demand and supply ? In the main, the problem arises from the fact that demand is too volatile for supply, or alternatively, that the supply of goods and services cannot adjust itself with sufficient rapidity to changes in demand. There are, therefore, two sides to the problem, two avenues of approach to the solution. One is to prevent demand from fluctuating so violently. The second is to speed-up the process of adjustment of supply.

Demand fluctuates, as we have seen, in two ways. The total volume of demand for all goods and services is considerably larger at some times than at others. Secondly, the particular varieties of goods and services demanded change from time to time. Now, in general, there is no reason why we should *want* to restrict or limit changes in the *variety* of demand. Mere fickleness of fashion, it is true, causes a great deal of economic waste and should be discouraged, so far as it is possible to do so without dictating what people shall buy—which would hardly be consistent with a democratic economy. But the more important changes in the variety of demand are precisely the ways in which progress shows itself. It would have been wrong a hundred years ago to discourage the community from suddenly demanding railways instead of stage coaches. It would have been equally wrong in our own time to have prevented the shift in demand from railway transport to road transport. Doubtless, if such shifts in demand were prevented, the regularity of the economic system would be greatly increased. But by the same action we should be petrifying the standard of living at its present level. Progress necessarily involves change. A continuous change in the variety of demand is a necessary condition of economic progress. We can rightly try to limit the inconveniences it causes. But we shall interfere with the process itself only at the cost of obstructing the path that leads to plenty for all.

These considerations do not apply to the fluctuations in the *volume* of demand, which are almost entirely a loss to the community. We shall be fully justified in trying to iron them out. Much the most important cause of fluctuations in the volume of demand is the tendency of the community to crowd its construction of capital goods into one half of the trade cycle. It is easy to see why fluctuations originate in the demand for capital goods. People's demand for consumption goods does not vary very much unless it is compelled to. Once a family has accommodated itself to a certain standard of living it will not suddenly make up its mind to consume less, unless it is forced to. It follows that fluctuations in the demand for consumption goods do not originate trade cycles; they follow from other causes. But very large fluctuations in the demand for capital goods originate quite independently of the community's ability to buy them. And when the demand for capital goods falls off, the capital goods makers have to tighten their belts and demand fewer consumption goods.

Broadly speaking, if we could eliminate the fluctuations in the demand for capital goods, the fluctuations in the demand for all other sorts of goods would take care of themselves.

How, then, are we to reduce the fluctuations in the demand for capital goods? The most promising way seems to be to develop a skilled and elastic technique for influencing the private decisions of those who have capital to invest. At times their willingness to buy capital goods needs stimulating, at times it needs reining in.

We are in the difficult position in this matter that while a very great deal has been written about the subject, comparatively little has been actually done by way of practical experiment. The chief need of the present is for more laboratory experiments rather than for more theorising. Accordingly, no attempt will be made here to do more than indicate some of the methods that have been suggested for controlling the volume of new investment in fixed capital.

The most obvious method, and the one that is likely to be most effective, since it affects simultaneously the whole field of savings and investment, is control of the rate of interest at which money can be borrowed for capital purposes, or, alternatively, at which the intending purchaser of capital goods can instead put his money into existing securities. Clearly, the lower the rate of interest the more capital investment there will be, and the higher the rate of interest the less capital investment there will be. There are plenty of examples in financial history of the volume of new investment being arrested by an increase in the rate of interest. The cheap money policy in Great Britain in the years after 1932 seems to provide evidence of the ability of a striking reduction in the rate of interest to stimulate investment. There is undoubtedly a big field for the development of conscious control over private investment by manipulation of the rate of interest.

It has frequently been suggested that the rates of taxation levied on the sums that companies put aside for replacing their fixed capital as it wears out might be varied in such a way as to encourage companies to do their replacement in years when there is a slack demand for capital goods. It is a promising idea, but so far as I know, no conclusive experiment on these lines has ever been tried. It should be.

Or again, suggestions have often been made that a National Investment Board should be set up to control the flow of money into capital investment. There is no doubt that such a Board, equipped with the requisite powers, could effectively limit an excessive volume of investment. It seems much more questionable whether it would be successful in summoning up an adequate volume of private investment when none was naturally forthcoming.

All these are ways in which the community, acting through the state and the public authorities, can try to influence the volume of investment by private persons and companies. But if they are not successful in producing a greater regularity of demand for capital goods, it is always open to the state itself to step into the breach. The state always has certain work of a capital nature to do—roads to make, public buildings to construct, battleships to build, etc.—and the argument seems to be incontrovertible that it should concentrate as much as possible of this work into the years when the private demand for capital goods is low.

Whether the state should go any further and set out, in bad years, to do a greater volume of capital works than is necessary on a mere consideration of the needs of the administrative machine is more doubtful. It has been most authoritatively urged, and in some countries the public works policy has been very successful. In others, the advantages have been less obvious—either because the necessary borrowing frightened the capital market and drove up the rate of interest, or because the public works were concentrated on too narrow a range of industries, or for other reasons.

In all these ways, however, there is a need for the community to feel its way towards a technique of controlling the total volume of investment, public and private alike. Where the objective has been so clearly defined, and so much thought has been devoted to methods, it would be entirely unreasonable to suppose that we shall not be able to achieve some successes in limiting the enormous wastes of the present senseless fluctuations from boom to slump in our demand for the machines that help us to produce wealth. The one device that has never failed to produce full employment is the waging of, or the full-scale preparation for, war. We need to find a method of creating productive capital that will be as effective as the accumulation of weapons of destruction.

4

The stabilization of demand, on the lines discussed in the preceding section, is the more promising approach to the problem of diminishing irregularity. But that does not by any means imply that nothing can be done on the side of supply. The problems are here, of course, reversed. The trouble arises because demand is too volatile, flighty, and fast-moving, and because supply is too stodgy and slow to budge. The solution is to slow down the fluctuations of demand and to speed up the reactions of supply. We must now turn to the possibilities of remedial action in this second half of the problem.

Both capital and labour are hard to move once they

have been "fixed" in a given occupation. That part of capital that is represented by buildings can sometimes change its employment; a derelict typewriter factory can be used for making sewing machines. But there are obvious limits to even this minor degree of transferability of capital. Moreover, capital sunk in the form of machinery is usually almost incapable of being used for any but the intended purpose — and tends to get more so as machinery becomes more complicated and specialized. Broadly speaking, capital cannot be transferred. In this respect, capital is less favourably placed than labour. But capital has its own remedy. It is usually possible to foresee at least approximately not merely the physical life of a piece of machinery but also its economic life (*i.e.* the period during which it can be employed more profitably than a newer machine), and the wise capitalist makes provision for depreciation to cover the cost of replacing the machine as soon as its economic life is over.

Few workers are able to accumulate funds to offset the eventual disappearance of their economic value through sheer old age, let alone the sudden "obsolescence" due to economic changes. Moreover, the transferability of labour from one industry to another is very limited, especially when it involves transfer from one locality to another. It is largely confined to the young and to the unskilled fringes. Anything that the community can do to make transfer easier—by an extension of the Labour Exchange system, by provision for re-training workers in declining industries to give them new skills, by grants to cover the costs of moving families from one district to another, etc., etc.—will be repaid to it in a greater elasticity of the whole economic system. But it is only fair to say that the various devices that have been tried along these lines in the past two decades have so far achieved no major successes.

Even if we cannot get very far in increasing the positive aids to transfer, we can at least see that we refrain from putting obstacles in its way. Actually, many aspects of action by the Government or the community in recent years might have been deliberately designed to impede transfer. We have done things which tend to keep labour and capital attached to dying industries instead of encouraging them to move away. And if labour or capital does leave its previous occupation, there is a growing list of obstacles to starting up in a new trade.

Many of these impediments—especially those of the first kind, which encourage labour and capital to cling to their declining industries—are the direct result of the community's kindliness. Unemployment insurance and assistance, for example, seem to us now to be but an elementary expression of Society's obligations to its less fortunate members. But it cannot be denied that they have very considerably dulled the keenness of the urge to set out in search of new varieties of work. Uncomfortable though the dole may be, it is considerably more comfortable than nothing at all. But when this difficulty is sought to be removed by a provision making it possible to exclude a man from benefit if he is "not genuinely seeking work," there is a sharp, and justified, protest on humanitarian grounds. This is a dilemma to which no solution has yet been found ; the community must find some way by which the urge to seek work remains in all its intensity, without inflicting starvation upon the unemployed. The problem is immensely complicated at present by the fact that wages (in many trades) and the dole are almost the same in amount, especially for a man with a large family, while neither, for such a man, is far above the starvation line. When wages have been so far increased that it will be possible to fix a level of dole payments that is considerably below wages and yet above the Irreducible Minimum, the problem will be well on the way to solution.

Further examples of mistaken kindness are to be found in some of the legislative devices for helping depressed industries. Coal is the best instance. Coal in modern Britain is certainly a declining industry in the sense that there is no prospect (in 1939) of there being sufficient demand to employ all the pits or all the miners attached to the industry. The state, by the Coal Mines Act of 1930 and the subsequent legislation, adopted the solution of compulsorily spreading the available demand for coal over the largest possible number of pits and men, so that the whole industry tends to be half-employed. This has several disadvantages. It prevents the most efficient mines from working full-time and producing coal for the community at the cheapest possible price. Secondly, the tight control of production that is necessary to work the quota scheme enables the industry to exact a monopoly price. But thirdly, and most relevantly to our present purpose, it encourages scores of thousands of men to hang on in the industry, living partly on inadequate wages, partly on the dole. It would have been much sounder policy for the community to have concentrated the production of coal where it could be done most cheaply, and to have allowed those mines to work with all the economies of full time, and to have deliberately pensioned off, as an act of charity, the mines and the men left derelict. Once again, we have to find a means of diminishing the pains of progress by helping unemployed men, without impeding the progress itself by insisting on retaining as coal miners men who no longer have any economic justification for plying that trade. That sounds like a hard saying. Perhaps it is; but not all true and necessary things are pleasant. We must bring ourselves to realize that the man who, by a quota scheme or a subsidy, is kept working half-time in an inefficient mine, is actually costing the community more than if he were maintained in idleness, and helped to find another trade.

These are examples of the community's efforts to prevent people leaving declining industries. Further examples could be given of the restrictions that are placed on the entry of both labour and capital into expanding industries. There is a whole host of quite unnecessarily restrictive trade union regulations, designed to create conditions of remunerative scarcity for particular varieties of skill, which stand in the way of the man who wants to change his job. Some of the higher castes of skilled labour are almost hereditary. Trade union regulations also frequently impede the entry of fresh capital into an industry where it could serve the community by increasing efficiency. In some trades, for instance, a new machine may not be installed unless as many men are (quite unnecessarily) employed on it as were employed on the machine it replaces. This provision, in many cases, removes the whole point of introducing the new machine, since it is the very essence and quintessence of mechanical progress that it saves labour.

The greatest restrictions on the free movement of capital, however, come from the side of capital itself. There is a short but growing list of trades which a new-comer is prevented *by law* from entering. There is a considerably longer list of trades which a new-comer will *in fact* find it impossible to enter. These restrictions are imposed, of course, in order to buttress the incomes of the capital and labour already within the charmed circle. And it goes without saying that their effect is anti-social —doubly so, in fact, since they provide the opportunity (seldom rejected) for monopoly exactions, and since they diminish the elasticity with which the system of supply can be expanded to meet new demands. Another instance of the same pernicious principle at work can be seen when an established industry, threatened with competition by a new industry, attempts to throttle its competitor's development. Some of the restrictions that have been imposed upon the development of road transport are doubtless necessary on their own merits. But, beyond question, some of them have been imposed to protect the railways—both the stockholders' capital and the railwaymen's jobs.

All these are difficult questions. The ideal solution is to be found neither in saying that competition must be unrestricted and the weak must go to the wall (since that leads to untold distress and disorder) nor in protecting the profits and wages of every stockholder or worker who is threatened by progress (since that leads to a petrified economy, which could neither increase the standard of living of its members nor prevent the growth of great stagnant pools of unemployment). The solution lies in finding means of clearing the path for the most rapid and ruthless change, while doing all that is necessary to compensate or succour the victims. It might be proper to tax the profits of the young and expanding to help the old and declining ; it would at least be less improper than to prevent them from expanding or earning any profits at all.

There is no other economic problem to which less thought has been given, and more should be given, than this problem of speeding-up the process of change. It is a matter that requires the accumulation of practical devices rather than the elaboration of theoretical principles—so the economists have neglected it. And the "practical" men are usually wrapped up in the affairs of this or that particular interest. It is a matter for a race of men that we have not yet learned to breed : the economic statesmen who, within the bounds of the practical and the possible, can yet see the interests of the community complete and in full perspective.

5

The solution of the problem of Regularity has just been described as " the accumulation of practical devices." Let it be frankly admitted that this is an unsatisfactory answer to have to give to one of the most insistent demands of the modern world. The analogy between diseases of the human body and defects of the economic body has been used many times in this book, and it is illuminating in this connection too. For some diseases the doctor can prescribe a single specific and be confident of its success—as insulin for diabetes or inoculation for hydrophobia. But there are other diseases—cancer, tuberculosis, and many others—where there is either no known single cure, or else the treatment is composed of a great variety of stringent rules of life. In these latter cases, the doctor who claims to have a simple sovereign specific is a quack. So in the economic field it is, in the present state of our knowledge, perfectly consistent to put forward (as has been done in this book) cures which are fundamentally simple for two of the three great economic diseases and yet confess that there is no single cure for the third. For poverty the solution is capital ; for inequality the solution is the limitation of inheritance. For irregularity we have suggested no more than a collection of salves and dressings, without much confidence that they will be efficacious.

Before we leave the subject in this unsatisfactory condition, however, we must take account of the fact that there are very many people who believe they know a simple and effective solution to the third problem of irregularity, as well as the other two. This solution is in a great many different ways of manipulating money.

The subject of money has been very largely ignored in this book. The omission has been deliberate. Money is, indeed, a subject of extreme importance. But one of the major misfortunes of economic discussion in recent years is that economists and the public have tended to become so engrossed in the details of monetary policy that they have forgotten the economic realities underlying money. This book was deliberately planned to get down to the bedrock of economic fundamentals. Money, after all, is only a garment or a screen, and if a thing is not economically feasible, money cannot make it so.

This proposition, however, has an obverse side. If a thing is economically possible it should not be held up for lack of finance. This is the truth that lies behind the advocacy of all the monetary reformers in all their hues and all their degrees of sobriety or phantasy. Before we can finish with our subject we must first explore what aid can be expected from money and monetary policy in maintaining the regularity of the economic system. To do so, however, is a difficult task, for no economic subject is so beset with obscurities and littered with controversies. The only method possible in our few remaining pages is to state briefly and with inevitable dogmatism what seems to be the truth, and leave the full reasoning that lies behind to be developed at length on another occasion.

Most projects of " monetary reform " boil down, on examination, to a proposal for an increase in the supply of money by giving or lending newly created money either to everybody or to some specific class of persons. This is a proposition to which it is not possible to give a blanket Yes or No. The answer can only be that an increase in the supply of money is always wrong if done to excess, but sometimes right if done in moderation. There is no doubt that an increase in the supply of money tends to increase the demand for capital goods. If it occurs during a period of depression it thus tends to inject an additional element of demand where it is most needed. The danger of money-injection is that it leads to *too much* demand for capital, which attracts into the capital-producing industries more resources of labour and capital than can be permanently kept busy there.

Depression times, therefore, provide the best case for increasing the supply of money. On the other hand, it would be very hard to find a set of circumstances in which an actual reduction in the supply of money would be justified. Consequently, the conclusion seems to be that the supply of money should be increased in each depression, and kept stable in each period of prosperity. The *average* tendency would be towards a slow increase in the supply of money and an equally slow rise in prices.

This recommendation can be justified both on theoretical and historical grounds. An increasing supply of money, exchanging against a stable supply of goods (or at least a supply of goods increasing more slowly than the money), leads to higher prices. And a period of rising prices is one in which the business man, the *entrepreneur*, the profit-receiver, gains at the expense of other classes of the community. The sums he pays out for wages or interest on loans are fixed by contract, at least for periods at a time, and if the prices at which he sells rise, his margin of profit is increased. Any one who has followed the argument of this book will readily see that a rise in the average level of profits will lead to increased industrial activity and, in particular, to heavy investment of capital. The worker with fixed wages and the lender with fixed interest tend during such a period to lose through the rise in prices. But they gain in the security of their incomes, and they gain also from the greater wealth of the community that is made possible.

A second reason for desiring a gradual and steady rise of prices is to get rid of the burden of dead-weight debt. Every community is burdened not only with the interest on its capital (*i.e.* on its active, useful, wealth-creating fixed plant), but also with the interest on its debt (*i.e.* the monetary obligations that embody the losses of the past). The lower the burden of debt, the more elastic and productive will industry be. One way of getting rid of debt is default. Another is a fall in the value of the money in terms of which the debts are payable (*i.e.* a rise in prices). There are very few generations in economic history that have not chosen one or the other. And of the two a rise in prices is infinitely the less disturbing. In nearly every century but the nineteenth the supply of money has steadily increased, the average level of prices has steadily risen, and the real burden of dead-weight debt has been steadily reduced. The nineteenth century could afford to be the super-honest exception, because it happened to be a period when the combined effect of rapidly increasing population and the first fruits of the Industrial Revolution was to set in train so powerful a tendency towards economic expansion that purely monetary expansion was not necessary as a stimulant. We are not so fortunate as our Victorian fathers. We shall need a rising level of prices both to rescue us from the depressions into which we shall fall, and to reduce the debt-burden that these depressions will leave behind.

In the world as it is, the effect of money is probably to increase rather than to diminish the instability of the economic system. The supply of money tends to be increased in boom times and diminished in slumps, and in both cases it merely accentuates the swing of the pendulum. It artificially enhances profits when they are already too large, and diminishes them when they are already too small. But it should not be beyond the wit and ingenuity of bankers to reverse this process and harness the powerful agency of money to the task of increasing regularity. Money will never be, can never be, the miraculous cure-all that the witch-doctors of monetary reform would have us believe. But given moderation in monetary strategy and skill in its tactical management, money has a very great contribution to make to the wealth and happiness of mankind.

INDEX

INDEX

PRINTED IN GREAT BRITAIN AT
THE PRESS OF THE PUBLISHERS
219